Y0-DKL-907

Joy Comes in the Morning
Overcoming Adversity

By
Sherri K. Baldwin

Joy Comes in the Morning
By Sherri K. Baldwin
Copyright: 2011

First Printing 2011

Editor//Cover Design: Mandi Jarvis
Cover Photography: Tammy Tran

ISBN: 978-1456583484

For additional information on books by Sherri Baldwin or to
invite the author to speak to your group or company, contact:

LeadAdvantage, Inc.

info@leadadvantageinc.com
www.leadadvantageinc.com

Table of Contents

Acknowledgments

This book has been a long time in the writing. Originally I felt that writing would be therapeutic for me and then I kept feeling an urge from the Lord to complete the book. I finally listened.

I want to thank Mid, Julia's husband, for also supporting the printing of this book and agreeing to let me include the emails, Julia's speeches, pictures, and their names. May this study book be a blessing to him, touch the hearts of all who read it, and may it be an inspiration from the Lord.

I would also like to thank my friends, Lauri Thompson who spent time reading my rough draft and providing input and grammatical suggestions, along with Van Walton who encouraged me and provided wisdom both for the book and life. Mandi Jarvis, who has been a huge support and fan during the publishing process, and my dear friend Pastor Dawn Hand, who reviewed the scripture uses for accuracy. Finally, thank you, to my loving husband who stands by my side each and every day.

Dedicated in loving memory of my dear friend,
Julia Middleton

Joy Comes in the Morning
Overcoming Adversity

By
Sherri K. Baldwin

Introduction

"Weeping may come for the night, but joy comes in the morning. In my darkest hour, I (Julia) had open chest surgery. The surgery wasn't successful. Two hours into a ten-hour surgery, the doctor told my husband and father that the tumor had wrapped around my pulmonary artery and he sewed me back up. Unfortunately, I was still bleeding internally and in my darkest hour I could barely gasp for a breath and felt like I was drowning. At 4:30am, the nurse asked if I wanted to have my husband called in. Mid ran from the hotel to the hospital and only with my eyes could I plead for him to help me. I was slipping away and I knew it. Thankfully, he took control of the situation. He called in the doctor, who performed surgery and here I am. This is not the story; it was the situation. Fill in the blank of your adversity. The story is what he emailed to our friends and family that day: *Trust God – lean on Him – give Him all the glory, no matter what. Trust in Him and there will always be a better outcome than you can possibly imagine. 1*

Joy Comes in the Morning

Thessalonians says, 'to be joyful always, pray continually, and give thanks in all situations.' In other words, control your emotions or your emotions control you. You can go there, you just can't stay there. There is no life there and not at all where God wants you to be."

The above paragraphs are from a speech my dear friend Julia once gave on the subject of Adversity.

While Julia lay in intensive care after surgery, I stood quietly praying at her bedside. In an intense moment I will never forget, she woke up, pulled me close to her and with great effort, whispered in my ear, "Joy comes in the morning." Julia's words that day came from Psalm 30.

Psalm 30: 4-5

**"Sing to the Lord, all you godly ones!
Praise His Holy name.
His anger lasts for a moment,
But His favor lasts a lifetime!
Weeping may go on all night,
But joy comes in the morning."**

Did you notice, in the psalm, and in Julia's darkest hour, weeping precedes joy?

Introduction

The psalmist urges us to sing praise through the tears and joy will eventually come. Praising God during times of adversity seems ludicrous. During times of bad health, struggles in relationships, conflict at work, those times where we just can't see a light at the end – to **praise** Him? Singing praise when we are fighting to "keep the faith" is not an easy task. How do we remain hopeful when desperately trying to figure out why we deserve this battle in life?

In our darkest hour, how do we trust God and overcome our adversity? By choosing to believe the grace of God is bigger than our current situation, we will experience the peace of God despite our circumstance. Suffering is not due to God's anger for some past sin. As Julia quoted in the Psalm, His anger lasts only for a moment. So what takes its place? Grace. What a wonderful world this would be if we all lived our lives with grace. The world would be a better place if we could let go of anger and replace that emotion with love and forgiveness and extend grace to others. God loves each one of us, and as His children we are promised, **"His favor lasts a**

lifetime." **(Psalm 30)** The battle has already been won.

Lesson One: WHY ME?

"By wisdom a house is built, and through understanding it is established."
Proverbs 24:3

We have been stomping our feet and asking "why" since we were old enough to talk.

When unsatisfied with the answer, we simply ask louder and with increased persistence: "why, why, why? I want to know why, and I want to know now!" Inevitably, a frustrated parent responds with "because I said so." Into adulthood we go, asking why, occasionally rebelling along the way to the "because I said so" line of thinking, until we reach that wonderful age where we have all the answers. Then adversity strikes again and we realize that we truly don't have all the answers; get frustrated and are expected to be content with not always receiving the answers that we want. Not surprisingly, we relate to God in the same way. We get angry and ask "why me?" Then we stomp our feet and ask again with an increased sense of urgency, or occasionally rebelling until we realize, or resign ourselves to the fact that we may never understand why.

I have another theory though. I believe we grow by asking "why". Questioning things we do not understand

1

impels us to pursue answers, which in turn causes us to learn
and grow. Children learn by asking questions and listening
to the answers. Adults learn by asking questions and then
seeking answers. Think about it, scientists solve problems by
questioning and testing theories, business leaders question
results to get better results in the future, and personal
knowledge is gained by asking questions. Asking why bad
things happen or why we are in a particular situation leads us
to reflect, to seek God for wisdom, and therefore to grow. It
is those that never question who will never find true
understanding. Notice I did not say answers. That part is
true. We may not get the answer we so desperately want, but
we grow in understanding of God and trust in our God who
does have all of the answers.

In the following testimony Julia reveals her questions
and the wisdom that came from them:

"I went to the doctor due to shortness of breath. I
asked for antibiotics, but got a lot more than that! I was
diagnosed with a rare cancer called Thymoma; Stage four,
the latest stage. For those who are medically challenged like
I was, that means it was attached to my thymus gland. (The
thymus gland assists in the development of the immune
system and it tends to atrophy in adults.) I must have had it
for several years because it was now the size of a man's fist

on my chest bone and had grown into my chest cavity and around my lung.

Although many questions filled my mind at that moment, I only had one issue: why? I was led to read about Job and the awful struggles he went through; he lost his family, his wealth, and his health. Job's greatest test was not the pain and suffering, but that he did not know why he had to go through all of that. I can relate to that guy! I'd been very healthy, I didn't smoke, I exercised, took vitamin C, and I am a Christian.

So many Christians say, "I'll finish my course," but it is with misery and everyone around them is miserable. They say, "God, why are you doing this to me?" They say, "Okay, if this is God's will, okay, but I want to know *why.* When I get to heaven I've got some real questions and I want some real answers."

I heard this on a tape by Dan McLean, "Here's an idea: heaven should have an arena for those who have questions and it would be packed out to the max. To help answer the questions, there is a committee of people like John the Baptist who got his head cut off, or Isaiah (who they believe is the prophet in Hebrews) who was sawed in two, Peter who was crucified upside down, Stephen who was stoned to death, Moses who wandered around for 40 years in the wilderness, or maybe like Hannah who was childless. They'll be easy to pick out – John holding his head, Peter upside down, etc."

Just imagine. Can you imagine? "Okay, Julia is up next to ask her question." "Okay, I wanna' know why I got a tumor." John would comment, "What did she say? I lost my head and you are crying about a tumor." Isaiah says, "I'm still trying to get up." You get my point, I think.

It was then when I realized that our greatest test may be that we trust God's goodness even though we don't understand why our lives are going a certain way. We must learn to trust in a God that is good and not in the goodness of life. There will never be a place that God will lead you that the grace of God cannot keep you."

Julia's questions led her to greater trust in God and a deeper understanding of His grace.

ASK
Describe a time you have asked, "Why Lord?" Did you grow from that experience? In what way?

_____

_____

Pray now as a group or individual for wisdom and growth as a result of your question.

Lesson One: WHY ME?

Julia's questions led her to remember and to study the book of Job and the pain and suffering he experienced. More than the loss and suffering, Job was tormented with the question, "why"? Julia realized that she could agonize over the "why me" dilemma or she could live victoriously despite her pain and suffering. She chose the latter.

Reading the book of Job feels as if we are reading someone's private journal...in a way, we are.

FOR FURTHER STUDY, READ JOB 1-5 AND 38-42.

This book wrestles with the age-old question, "Why do righteous men and women suffer if God is a God of love and mercy?" Bad things happen to good people and often blaming God is the result. When our world crumbles and crises strike, what should we do? Job's life gives us an example to follow.

God considered Job "perfect and upright," and yet Job tumbled from prosperity to poverty. Today it might be similar to losing everything in the stock market and going from wealth and status to scraping by from paycheck to paycheck. The struggle was not between Job and God but rather between God and Satan. Satan argued that Job only honored God because he was so blessed with riches and respect, and that if God allowed him to take that away Job would become unfaithful. So God allowed Satan to destroy all Job had. Not because of anything Job had done but because God knew Job to be righteous not because of his prosperity but because of his heart. Job's wife added pressure by saying Job should curse God and die rather than go through all of the pain and suffering (Job 2:9), but Job stood firm in his faith, **"Shall we indeed accept good from God, and shall we not accept adversity." (vs. 10)** Job Chapter 3 begins a dialogue between Job and his friends who have good intentions when they come to him to provide support and offer suggestions for what might have caused his suffering. They reason his suffering must be due to some past sin he has committed (Job 4:7), but Job adamantly refutes that reasoning. Eventually, he wrestles with his own emotions and the question why, "I cannot understand it. It doesn't seem right." Job hits rock bottom, whining and complaining to God. Then he finally repents.

He eventually realizes that God is God, **"Though He slay me, I will hope in Him." (Job 13:15)** Job did not understand the reason for his suffering, yet he remained steadfast in his belief in a God who had the right to allow trouble and suffering in our lives as well as good. Job says to God, **"I know you can do anything," (Job 42:2)** and in

Lesson One: WHY ME?

verse 6 he falls to his face to pray. In the end of this emotional book, God blesses Job with double prosperity; he receives twice what he lost financially plus he finds happiness again with the blessing of a new family, but only after he suffered much pain and loss. The fact that his fortune was restored provides comfort; however, the greater richness came from his renewed perspective of God and his deep contentment from truly grasping the majesty of God.

God allows us to experience situations that we do not fully comprehend and may never understand, but we need to know that pain is not necessarily punishment; rather, it is just the price we pay for living in a fallen world. The good news is we are just passing through on our way to our permanent home with the Lord one day. Trusting God makes the journey much more exciting and definitely more bearable during the tough times.

Job's faith in the midst of adversity led to prosperity double-fold, more than he could have ever imagined. **Zechariah 9:12, also references receiving double-fold for our troubles, "Return to the stronghold, O prisoners who have the hope; this very day I am declaring that I will restore double to you."** God wants us to be so locked up in hope, expecting something good to happen, that we just

7

absolutely cannot doubt. Then He promises to bless us twice as much as we desire. Job learned many lessons through his adversity and he grew as a result, and lived a long and prosperous life.

ASK   Is there an area of your life that you could use God's blessings double-fold?

_____

_____

> **Pray through Zechariah 9:12 out loud several times. Between each prayer allow for individuals to call out a word or thought that stands out to them. Let God lead your thoughts as you pray and cling to His Word.**

In times of suffering, we need to trust God for wisdom and peace. The only way I know how to do that is on my knees in prayer with my mouth shut and my heart open. It is the only way I know to keep from getting bitter or negative. God will "sift us" if necessary to accomplish His greater purpose for our lives. His plans are far grander than ours. Guard yourself against negative thoughts by meditating and memorizing God's Word. It is imperative to replace negative thoughts with positive thoughts. When our minds are left unguarded they will run wild with imagination and false thoughts that will eventually sink us into a pit of despair. **Romans 12:2 says that the battle is in our mind and we should be, "transformed by the renewing of our mind."** (Ephesians 6:13-17 NLT) states, **"Put on the full armor of God…stand firm then, with the belt of truth buckled around your waist, the breastplate of righteousness in place, and with your feet fitted with the readiness that comes from the gospel of peace. In addition to all this, take up the shield of faith, with which you can extinguish all the flaming arrows of the evil one. Take the helmet of salvation and take the sword of the Spirit, which is the Word of God."** Without constantly putting on the "armor of God" to help us through tough times; where do we turn when we can't answer "why?"

The armor the world offers is not strong enough to protect us.

I know personally many times I have asked, 'Why, Lord,' for things much less significant than cancer. I have asked why God didn't bring me the man of my dreams until I was almost 40 and I had to deal with the heart-wrenching pain of loneliness. I have asked why I had to wait for a job to come along after a long period of unemployment and struggles of how I would pay the bills. I have asked why bad things happen to good people and good things happen to bad people. I have asked why family members or friends have had to suffer through health issues, career frustrations, shattered dreams, and broken relationships. Why is God taking so long to answer, and when He does answer, why it isn't the answer I expected? Why does tragedy and heartache affect Christians with the same intensity as the most evil people on earth?

When something negative happens, my first thoughts are cynical and self-defeating. My friends usually validate my feelings. As an example, I was a sales manager at a hotel for many years. A co-worker began stealing contracts off my desk after hours and submitting them as her own. My boss would not resolve the issue. I began to behave like the victim that I believed I was. As the tension rose in the office and associates took my side, they fueled the fire. I became angry with my co-worker, my boss and God for my situation. I felt sorry for myself and asked, 'Why is this happening to me when I don't deserve it? Why doesn't my co-worker get fired for stealing my business? God, why don't You fix this situation?' However, I knew in my heart what I needed was the armor of God and his belt of truth instead of my self-imposed anger.

ASK   How have you typically responded to friends who are struggling? Do you tend to give them "more fuel for their fire" or gently turn them to God who has all of the answers?

_____

_____

_____

> **Discuss or meditate on the meaning of Proverbs 15:14, "The mind of the intelligent seeks knowledge, but the mouth of fools feeds on folly."**

I began to pray for victory and cling to God's promises. I refused to let negative thoughts into my mind. I memorized scripture and repeated it out loud when the "what if's" tried to squeeze me with fear. 'What if I get fired? What if it never gets better? What if this is more than I can bear?' I repeated, **"Consider it all joy, my brethren, when you encounter various trials, knowing the testing of your faith produces endurance. And let endurance have its perfect result, that you may be perfect and complete lacking in nothing. But if any of you lacks wisdom, let** him ask of God, who gives to all men generously and without reproach, and it will be given to him. But let him ask in faith without a doubt, for the one who doubts is like the surf of the sea, blown, and tossed by the wind." (James 1:2-6) I refused to allow doubt to enter my mind and stay.

Once I abandoned my right to be RIGHT, or at least the temptation to argue about being right, God performed a miracle. He gave me peace in the midst of turmoil. He changed my heart. Then, God changed the heart of my co-worker. Notice that God gave me peace during the conflict first, and then changed the situation. I still do not understand why I had to endure that difficult time in my life.

Faith is not, ever asking why. Faith is, knowing that God is good even when things don't make sense and we may not get the answers we want, when we want them. That work incident has changed the way I respond to everything! Instead of over-reacting to situations, I try to look to God first to ensure I am responding in a manner pleasing to Him.

In hindsight, I see that God wanted me to understand the circumstance should not determine my behavior. I asked why and God answered, although differently than I expected. I realized that I was letting my co-worker control my life and my contentment. Peace and contentment only come from the

Lesson One: WHY ME?

Lord and my circumstances have nothing to do with it. Go ahead and ask, why. Faith is not ever asking why.

ASK   Is there a time God has said, "NO" to you and you realized later that it was for your own good? Describe.

_____

_____

_____

God is the author of our life and our life story. It is a story filled with passion and questions, opposition and crisis, joy and singing, intrigue and learning, living and yes, even dying. We can be the hero or heroine of our story if we trust in a God who not only is good, he is GREAT! **Romans 8:37 says that, "in all these things we overwhelmingly conquer through Him who loved us."** Job was a man "after God's own heart" and yet he experienced some of life's greatest heartaches and losses; who became plagued with the "Why me?" question. I have learned to ruthlessly trust in God! He is the One who does have all of the answers; He is **The** answer.

ASK   Is there a time God changed your heart and
then He changed your circumstance for the better?
Describe.

_____

_____

ASK   What have you learned from this chapter? I
learned it is okay to ask "why" because it leads to
seeking for "The" truth and that truth can only be
found in God.

_____

_____

Lesson Two: WE ALL NEED A LOVE STORY

"Greet one another with a kiss of love."
1 Peter 5:14

Love and encouragement go hand in hand. When we love someone we genuinely want the best for that person and will provide encouragement wherever possible. Children crave love from their parents, always wanting to be held and affirmed when they accomplish something. As we get older, we seek that love and affirmation from our friends. As adults we turn to our spouse and job to fulfill this need. While I believe God provides all of these things for us to enjoy; He also puts individuals in our life to give us glimpses of His love. God is the only One who can completely fill that need for acceptance that each of us carry within us and ultimately fill the need for love. Julia received glimpses of God's love through her wonderful friends and adoring husband during trying times.

Julia endured three years of chemotherapy and experimental treatments before being informed surgery was her last option. The cancer had spread throughout most of the left side her body and was pushing on several vital organs. Doctors thought they could reduce her pain by removing a portion of the cancer, and hopefully control and attack the rest of the cancer with radiation and continued chemotherapy.

However, once they commenced with surgery, the doctors realized that the growth of the tumor now encompassed the main artery leading to her heart. After deliberation with her family, the doctors discontinued the surgery for fear of severing the heart muscle.

When I heard the diagnosis, I immediately flew from my home in Charlotte to New York to provide support and encouragement. During the flight, all I could think about was how she could remain optimistic when she woke up and heard that the tumor could not be removed? When I arrived, I witnessed a husband and wife completely loving each other while keeping a positive attitude. This led me to more fervently believe that joy truly does come in the morning.

ASK   Describe a time you have felt truly loved by someone else when going through a difficult time. What did they do that made you feel loved?

_____

_____

Lesson Two: *WE ALL NEED A LOVE STORY*

What follows is a love story from Mid, Julia's husband. It reveals dependence on God and the love of God in the midst of trials. Mid corresponded through email to a long list of Julia's friends to keep us informed of her progress while at the hospital in New York. *[The emails have not been altered other than minor spelling and removing some of the graphic details or confusing medical terms.]*

<u>**2003:**</u>

Message from Mid at 9:45 AM on Tuesday 10/21 -

Good morning. We are waiting to see her this morning. Her blood pressure is down and we need prayer for that. She is really sleepy. Last night she said "surgery would have been too easy." God has bigger things in store for her! She looks beautiful with her big loving eyes looking up at you, and smiles through the pain... Love you! Mid

Message from Mid at 11:26 AM on Tuesday 10/21 –

Julia's blood pressure is 96 over 53...very low. They are doing all they know to get her pressure up. They are only allowing 2 of us at a time to see her. She wants music so we have gotten a CD to play some Bocelli and inspirational music. All the family is here and we are walking in God's peace. She is hanging on...and her blood pressure and heart rate increase when we touch her. Pray for God's strength for

us and that she goes to a regular room by day's end! Much
love, Mid

Message from Mid at 3:31 PM on Tuesday 10/21 -
Julia is feeling better. At 3:00 she has more color, told a joke
and still cannot have anything to eat, though she is hungry.
Her blood pressure is 88 over 50 which must increase. We
have been rubbing her noggin' and her feet. She is not out of
the woods but she looks better than she did this morning.
Appreciate your prayer! Mid

Message from Mid at 9:46 PM on Tuesday 10/21 -
Good evening! Julia is smiling and perky in a visual sort of
way. Her blood pressure is 100 over 80, which is GOOD.
She is hungry but cannot eat until hopefully tomorrow. The
surgery has left a huge "J" on her body. She told the
surgeon, "Good thing my name is Julia!" It has been a roller
coaster ride for the family today. I thought we were going to
lose her this morning...she got BETTER! Thank you for all
your love!!!! Middy

Message from Mid at 6:57 AM on Wednesday 10/22 -
Julia has had a fighting night. She was having a great deal of
trouble breathing on her own and her CO_2 count was twice

the normal level. She asked me to come in at 4:00 a.m. In the hotel room I got the call and rushed over. Stroking her hair and giving her an ice chip every now and then. She smiles with her eyes. She wanted to be tilted on her left side to let gravity do its job and relieve the pressure on her good right lung. Fortunately or unfortunately they have put a ventilator and sedated her. She is fighting with a smile. She did have a look of desperation that broke me and I wept. But I have to stay strong for her so she does not see hopelessness. Lord, grant her strength + send some for me! Middy

Message from Mid at 11:49 AM on Wednesday 10/22 - They have decided to take her back in to surgery to relieve the blood clotting and relieve the pressure on her breathing. The whole Recovery Room was in a buzz. Spoke to both surgeons, signed the release form for the OK.

Her brother came in and took our 9th Wedding Anniversary picture; we always hold up both of our hands, smile and snap the shot. All the nurses watched and we agreed that we will look back on this one with a good laugh.

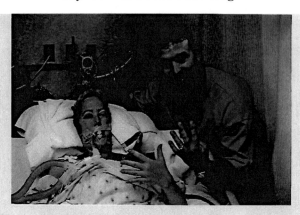

I whispered into her ear all the fantastic places we are going to travel to...Sailing Lake Cuomo in northern Italy on a clear harvest moonlit night, toasting Dom Perignon with crystal, private cove, beachside cabana 3-4 miles outside of a small Costa Rican village, snorkeling and eating tree-picked mangos, etc. I patted one of the Docs and said "get fired up...game time." The professional was calm and collected...he's ready.

She wanted to tell me something before she went in (for surgery) and had to use her finger to trace the letters. It said C-A-R-D. She has an anniversary card for me back at the hotel. Wow! What a doosey to read.

She gave me a look of confidence and a thumbs up as the surgery doors were shutting. God's peace is with her. Praise God! Glory to the Father. She is in the folks' hands and ALWAYS in God's hands.

Message from Mid at 1:40 PM on Wednesday 10/22 - Emotionally the family is drained riding the roller coaster, but it is medicating relief for me to share with you. Will update later...God Bless

Message from Mid at 5:15 PM on Wednesday 10/22 - Julia is resting like a new born baby.

She is on the ventilator, but they just lowered her oxygen level and they tell us that is good. :) Her corner room is private and a dimmed ray of light shines on her face. She is sedated and very peaceful with her breathing and her spirit. :) Her blood pressure is normal, Hallelujah!!!

Her high school cheerleading friends have come from Long Island to visit her. I told them to "talk to her, she can hear you." I left the room and they said she would occasionally raise her eyebrow in acknowledgement.

There is an angelic peace in her room. She breathes silently + peacefully. The light shining on her face illuminates her beauty. Angels are present. The Holy Spirit fills you with the knowing that everything is going to be all right.

We thank you for your prayers, the Lord is with her. Thank you! Thank you! Thank you!

She's going to be OK.

Joy Comes in the Morning

Message from Mid at 10:45 AM on Thursday 10/23

We cannot see her until 11:00 and some friends who came in from Chicago and Charlotte are eager to see and touch her. She has not eaten a thing since Sunday around 7:00pm! Bless her! The ICU doc said that young folks can hold off eating up to 5-7 days while waiting to get stable. They really haven't experienced Julia when she is hungry...better pray for that too! "It's not a pretty picture" Lon Chaney Style. Thanks Prayer Team for all your love...and bless all you serving Julia and the family.

Message from Mid at 6:10 PM on Thursday 10/23

Good news! Julia's CO_2 level is at 50 from 60 and 45-35 is normal.

She is in really great spirits and enjoying seeing the family and friends two at a time. She likes to sneak a drink from a sponge on a stick that is used to "moisten" her lips. Have to sneak around the nurses. They are going to keep her overnight in ICU and WILL MOVE HER TO HER ROOM TOMORROW!!!!! Yeah!!!

The family is in a joyous mood and talking about a cold beer and pizza at a New York pizza joint. Wow! Is it Thursday?

Lesson Two: WE ALL NEED A LOVE STORY

Thank you for your continued support! We feel your hands holding us up when we're low and hear your joy when we're up! Julia is stable and happy.

Much Love,

Middy + Family + Friends

Message from Mid at 1:45 PM on Friday 10/24 -
Unfortunately, the ICU team overrode the Doctor today. They are going to keep her in ICU. Pray for her lungs to clear.

The Doctor answered some of our questions today:

"No" to heart/lung transplant. If you have cancer "Forget about it!" Brooklyn Accent.

"Yes" to evaluating other possibilities to REDUCING the tumor. But as we know, surgery is not an option to getting the entire tumor, even with reduction. Reduction, though, could allow her to live a quality life.

Kissed her for the first time, and MAN did it feel GOOD! We have started receiving some flowers, cookies and love. We can only keep it in the ICU waiting room which is appreciated by ALL the loving relatives waiting there. We can move it all into her regular room when these cats feel comfortable in letting her go.

Going to see her now. Mom is with her and she likes a foot rub and rubbing her swollen left arm. The bath and clean hair has made her feel like a human again. The reality of the Doctor's analysis sunk in again and her eyes drooped low, but just for a second. Her dad breathed hope into her spirit about the "good" in the discussion. Her eyes lit up again. You all light up our eyes.

Message from Mid at 8:00 AM on Saturday 10/25
Arrived at hospital and snuck to her ICU room. Dang! She is still there...sleeping. We hoped she would have been moved to a room in the night, no phone call, but I was still hoping!
I bought some fresh cut mangos from a grocery store. NOT the grocery store you envision. These are open 24 hours, open aired to the street and smaller than your living room. Finally found a store near our hotel. That's the place to get breakfast. I have the mangos with me and I am going to the hospital cafeteria and get a knife. Gonna' cut the mango into little pieces and feed her around 8:30. Hee hee. Then I'm going to give her a back, noggin', + foot massage...love on her.
Beautiful NY morning! Crisp air, blue skies! When she is in transit to her room, going to sidetrack to the terrace.

Message from Mid at 11:00 AM on Sunday 10/26 -

We have a room! We put up 20+ 6" x 12" inspirational posters all around her walls. Words like "Dance", "Courage", "Faith", etc. They were done by family + friends on the 15th floor over the last couple days.

Also, we opened and read all the wonderful, uplifting cards. Really boosted her spirit!

The goal of recovery and home is for her to walk on her own, (She just did 2 laps around the floor with a standing cart!). She is on her way!

Julia's roommate is on pain medicine at all times and is having a bad go. Had a deep conversation with her loving husband about opening your heart to the Father and ask for his strength and peace. I relayed how that is how we know that everything is going to be OK, regardless of the circumstances. He shared that they were just having their 30 year anniversary + she is diagnosed with terminal lung cancer...9 months to live. He teared up and shared his heart. God is merciful. Pray for peace for them.

Thank you for all your love!

Message from Mid at 2:40 PM at 10/27 -

Julia is doing well in her room.

Good Things:

1) She is off the O2 when in her room. She still needs it when walking, though. Her walking O2 is 88% and needs to be over 93% to not need O2...thanks!

2) She is nibbling on all kinds of food, loves the pears that someone brought!

3) She has put ON weight. We were told that she would DEFINITELY lose weight and she defied that by 24 pounds! She may not have wanted me to tell you that one.

4) Her spirit is strong and the room is alive with happiness! Her Bible study girls pieced a passage of scripture together on posters and it is on the wall right beside her bed.

5) She is walking unassisted already. They have this awesome piece of equipment that assists people walking and she did not need it today.

6) She is so moved by all the love and prayer from all of you! She is so thankful that this challenge of life has been a testament to the loving, merciful grace of JEHOVAH through his Son Jesus Christ! All the prayer partners turning to him to answer their prayers! Such praise to GOD!

Things that need to get better:

1) Strength. Walking is OK, but she needs continued strength to lift herself up and go from chair to bed.

2) Appetite. More caloric intake.

3) Fluid Expulsion. Fluid buildup in her left leg, arms, sides etc. need to "flow" out of her body.

4) Other treatment possibilities. Meeting with radiologist Wednesday and will have heard back from Tucson by then. Boosts her spirit to "live" with the tumor and eventually killing it.

Good news today, her vitals have improved somewhat and the family is on an "up" today! I shared that friends would pray for peace for her and the family and they are uplifted and noticeably calmer!

Lots of folks in the main lobby again today. Surgery is done every day here for some kind of cancer. I look at their anxious + concerned faces and remember us a week ago. Feel like a veteran.

Yesterday Julia walked an assisted 1/2-mile! Amazing really! Today we are already at an unassisted ¼ mile. She needs more rest really...wants to entertain all the visitors. She got on me about not "being" with her. I did not understand what she meant; I've been with her virtually the whole time. She said "No! I mean being with me. You're here but you're not here!" I went to go to my cave and ate raw meat. Anyway, I asked her how can I be "Here, here?!?" She said "By loving me, touching me, holding me, massaging head + neck, and listening to me." I came out of my cave, dropped the fresh kill and said, "Oh! Ok, I can handle that!" I think all men have moments of "Huh?" with their woman, but relax, hold on, they will explain better and you will understand.

God bless you!

Message FROM JULIA at 10:29 AM on Wednesday 10/29 - GOOD MORNING WORLD!

I am looking out my window at a beautiful day; actually it's quite cloudy out, but any kind of Day is a beautiful day. While every day gets better, today is so much better. After a great night's sleep, up at 5:30am, I've already done some walking laps, lost 14 lbs from yesterday (did Mid tell you I gained over 30 lbs in less than a week - OY!), and have energy to leap tall buildings in a couple bounds. I had acupuncture for pain control & to help me sleep and today I get a lymph massage & reflexology on my feet and a makeover. (Did Mid say I was at the hospital or something crazy like that?)

Last night I did something I've always wanted to do: Paint. Heh Heh Heh. Four of my high school buddies came over and we went to the activities center and painted watercolor. It was so much fun, and then they turned our paintings into note cards. Tonight is Horseracing Bingo - anyone interested?

Thank you SOOO much for your notes, prayers, stories from home. Both Mid & I haven't felt like we were going through this alone with such an incredible, God-given network of friends.

Love,

Julia

Message FROM JULIA at 8:45 PM on Thursday 10/30

Hello from Club Med

Guess what folks – I've got my walking papers for tomorrow!! That means we are on taps to come home this SATURDAY!! WHOOP, WHOOP.

I'm not sure what sped up the process. I'm not sure if it is either that I'm doing well enough physically or that when my doctors made their rounds last night, my friends were dying my hair, posting magnetic Barbies on the wall, growing foam farm animals in water, while playing with crazy straws and play dough. Hmmmmm. Perhaps they needed this room for those who are really sick.

Much love to you!

Julia

Message FROM JULA late night on Friday 10/31

Bon Voyage NYC!

Checking out of Spa Sloan Kettering today gave me a lot of time to reflect on the last 2 weeks here. There are so many thoughts, mixed feelings, memories. Overwhelming, really. Yesterday was so beautiful because it was the first day outside in a week and a half. Friends took Mom & I to the outside patio of the activities floor and we played Scrabble until one of them won by getting 40 points with "QVC". Hunkering into a movie w/ popcorn, raisons, Jr. Mints® and Swizzles® marked my last night spent in the hospital. Only top shelf junk food for us girlies.

One friend ended up staying over and as we were talking late night, I found myself taking it all in- asking - what do I do now? I just now realized that I had never had a Plan B. I mean, there was never a question about NOT having a near complete surgical resection, so we never thought otherwise. The reality of it all just hit me.

The radiologist had come in that day and said that since we wanted to look at something closer to home, he would contact someone at Duke and see if they were up for the challenge of doing my radiation. Since it now covers such a large area (as opposed to if they could've removed most using surgery), it will be a challenge.

But then again.... I'm up for the challenge.

I'm heading out today realizing so many things:

- That this current weak state of the body is ONLY temporary.

- As I fearfully leave the safety net of doctors, I jump into a better woven safety net of me depending wholly, fully on God and our incredible friends & family at home.

- That my friends will understand when I break out into a deep, knee buckling, and hacky cough that all I really need is a good couple slaps on the back and I'll be ok again.

- That I SO look forward to finding out about what is happening in your lives.

- That I have the most wonderfully amazing husband and that up until a few days ago I had no idea he was so gifted at expressing himself by writing on this website. He is an absolute dream.

- NYC has the best costumes for Halloween.

- That Mid & I are the most blessed humans I know because of each one of you.

- God is so good that even when we cannot find the energy to pray for ourselves, He brings in others to help carry us.

- That is exactly what you have done for me.

I am in complete and total awe of His goodness,

Much love, Julia

Message from Julia on Thursday 11/5 (home) -

On the road to recovery - yeah!

What a great last few days! After a wimpy first day back, we have made great strides. I have mastered the end of the street, and tomorrow perhaps we'll be adventurous and try a cul-de-sac or two. Anyone who visits has to master the art of the kind back slap during coughing spells, but that will just bring us closer together.

We were sitting outside today (NC is absolutely showing off-it's so beautiful) and we were sharing funny stories from the last few weeks.

Did you hear about...? The day I was feeling particularly feisty and had a gown that had no tie back? My friends were walking me and as I would stroll down the hall, I would shrug my outside robe off - much to their horror. Let's say I was feeling particularly freeeee that day.

I asked you all at the beginning to save some champagne for me for the successful surgery, so instead, 6 of us opened a bottle to celebrate my first night in my real room. (And they thought cheating with the cantaloupe was bad!)

An older woman chaplain came to pray with the family before the first surgery and we were all quite serious and holding hands and teary. So she offered up her heartfelt prayer for.... her brother-in-law who was experiencing pain and then was praying about God being a faithful dog that walks by your side. During which several of us opened one eye and could hardly keep from laughing because it was the exact prayer our friend got when he had this surgery 3 years ago there!

Ah memories...

Looking forward to making lots more

Julia

Message from Julia on 11/26 -

I'M BAAAAAACK!!!!

They told me I should feel mostly back to normal after a month and sho' nuf they were right. The last four days or so I've gotten energy back and able to do a lot of things. The "J" scar has healed nicely, I'm on the infamous 'Rush' painkillers, so I don't really know if I have any pain, and with daily facials, massages and manicures, it really keeps me in top shape <grin>.

We have been so blessed over the last month to be able to spend really good quality time with members of our family and some dear friends. On a side note, from my one watercolor experience in NYC, I'm now going to sign up for a painting class in January. This is a far stretch for someone who preferred Excel spreadsheets and 'data analysis'. I'm not sure if this is a new me or I'm just a creative want-to-be. On the medical front, we have been thinking we would roll into radiation, but wasn't sure where (NY, TX or Duke?). Then some clinical trials came up at Duke that we are looking into. Once you do radiation, you don't qualify for most of the clinical trials available, so we're back to... "Try everything else out there...." These trials are for drugs that inhibit the blood supply of tumors, so it sounds interesting enough. We will know shortly if and when I will do a clinical trial.

I have been humbled to my knees by your prayers on our behalf. Someone asked what they could pray for specifically and it would probably be for wisdom during this decision-making time as well as to strengthen my personal relationship with God. He is the one who I am clinging to and even during these challenging times, still gives me so much JOY.

Thanks for your uplifting messages and prayers - I still feel them!

Julia

TWO Years Later (2005):

From: Mid

Sent: Friday, April 01, 2005 10:36 PM

Subject: Julia Update 4/1/05

Hello Brothers & Sisters! My heart is filled knowing you are there. Julia has had a rough time since the first of this year. Food poisoning, infected area in her chest cavity (required a drain for about 3 weeks), low blood pressure, accelerated heart rate, fevers, low immunity.

We learned today that her cancer has grown 15% this last month. She was in a clinical trial in Tucson, AZ & they must have been feeding cancer growth liquid.

Anyway, she IS out of the study & coming home to me tonight. They compared her CAT scans from a month ago with her current scan and determined that the tumor which has been around her heart and all over her left lung is now on her liver, her ovaries, & other spots in her abdomen. She has been in a lot of pain lately; the strong opiates have helped her manage. She is now on the "Poor Man's Drug" methadone & the pharmacist looks at her funny when she picks up her drugs (It is primarily used for heroin addicts). Ha! Anyway, her beautiful smell, smile, voice, and love are coming to me tonight. Back home to be with me. My gut ...my gut aches, tears are in my eyes remembering talking with her today, tasting her tears over the line. Why the suffering for such an angel? Why the suffering? Why the suffering? She said, "the positive is we can make plans now! We have been planning & putting off some exotic ports of call because of pain & discomfort flare-ups the past few months." She sees the light in even some disappointing news. Hey...my beautiful angel...............I love her.

I've been mad all day. Have asked for the Holy Spirit to bring his peace beyond ALL understanding to cradle the hearts of our families as they received the tough news today. I've been less faithful & full of pride, wanting to hurt something, feeling barbaric, not asking for peace for me.

Need to hear her, smell her, taste her, and cherish her when I
hold her tonight.

Then I will ask for peace. FOR IT COMES QUICKLY!!
Praise God!

We will make another game plan. Mix some goo with more
goo. She is run down now & weakened by this last regime.
Through prayer, rest, & service to her she will regain her
physical strength & fight on.

Julia has already won, she's been winning for years, and
she's a winner. Her faith is SO STRONG...mine now is
weak.

Pray for peace for me.

…And we all did for the next several years of ups and
downs. The Lord was faithful and provided that peace until
He finally took all of her pain away forever. On that day,
when He took her home to be with Him in Heaven, we truly
understood that Joy Comes in the morning.

These emails reveal Mid's love for Julia. We get a
glimpse of his heart, and her zest for life. Scripture is God's
love letter to you and me. We get a glimpse of God's heart
and it is good. It is an unshakable love. **"This is how much
God loved the world: He gave his Son, his one and only
Son. And this is why: so that no one need be destroyed;
by believing in him, anyone can have a whole and lasting**

life" (John 3:16, The Message). Whole and lasting, two
things we desperately seek but rarely find in this world. We
can find them in Christ.

Jesus demonstrated His love for us and gave us an
example to follow. Jesus was tested, rejected and received
criticism, just like many of us, and yet gathered strength from
God to withstand it all. Jesus prayed for us, and His enemies.
He even suffered crucifixion in order to save us from our sin.
Jesus is God's perfect impression and expression of love. His
life and death represent God saying to me and you, "I cherish
you. Be Mine."

God loves us so much that He gave us His most
valuable gift, His Son. After Jesus rose from the grave and
ascended back to heaven, God sent His Spirit to remain with
us. As He shares Himself with us through His Son and His
Sprit, God says, "You are my beloved."

Scripture reveals God and how much we are loved
and cherished. Read His words that He has given us through
the Bible; meditate and pray on them and God will reveal
Himself to you. Just like the apostle Paul prayed in
**Ephesians 3:18-19 (NLT), "May you have the power to
understand, as all God's people should, how wide, how
long, how high, and how deep His love is. May you
experience the love of Christ, though it is too great to**

understand fully. **Then you will be made complete with all the fullness of life and power that comes from God."**

"For the mountains may be removed and the hills may shake, but My loving kindness will not be removed from you, and My covenant of peace will not be shaken." **(Isaiah 54:10)**

Wow, that is so encouraging to me! God loves us so much he wants to give us peace and take away all of our tears. Scripture is His love letter to me…and you!

ASK   Is there a specific time you felt God's love in the midst of adversity? Thank Him for that love. Describe.

_____

_____

How do you know if God loves you? How do I know God loves me? I can see God's love all around me. I see it in other people, like Julia, and how the Lord has presented circumstances in my life in order to change me through the years. I see God's love through adversity, in the beauty of nature, and in the wonderful things He has done for me.

My parents divorced when I was seven. We were latchkey kids that were home alone most of the time. My brothers and I fought like most siblings do and learned how to fend for ourselves when needed. Then when I was in Junior High School my mom got a phone call from a friend that she had lost touch with after the divorce. The friend told my mom she had become a Christian and knew that she had not been there to support my mom during her time of need and broken my mom's trust. She also invited us to go to church with her. For the first time, I understood what forgiveness and God's love was all about. The more I learned about God and this unconditional love, the more I wanted to learn, and the more I fell in love with the Lord, Jesus Christ. That process has never stopped for me.

When I flew to New York in 2003 to see Julia, I witnessed God's love and provisions at every juncture. One of my clients provided a free airline ticket to New York. The hotel company I worked for at the time offered a free hotel room in New York. Another friend acted as chauffer from the airport so I didn't have to rent a car. The most amazing miracle, Julia woke up when I was in her room, as I mentioned in the Introduction, pulled me close and said, "Joy comes in the morning."

So my prayer for you is the same as Paul's in Philippians 1: 9-11 from The Message: "that your love will flourish and that you will not only love much but well. Learn to love appropriately. You need to use your head and test your feelings so that your love is sincere and intelligent, not sentimental gush. Live a lover's life, circumspect and exemplary, a life Jesus will be proud of; bountiful in fruits from the soul, making Jesus Christ attractive to all, getting everyone involved in the glory and praise of God." Repeat prayer in your own words.

ASK

Do you believe you "live a lover's life" as the text mentions above? Why or why not? What is one thing you can do to change that if you need to change? Describe.

_____

_____

Write a love letter to someone today and mail it. It can be someone going through a difficult time or just someone special to you. Tell them what they mean to you and why.

Lesson Three: MY HERO

"Let us therefore make every effort to do what
leads to peace and to mutual edification."
Romans 14:19

Do you remember the story of David & Goliath? Others tried to persuade David to conform to their way of fighting (traditional heavy armor and weapons), but all he needed to defeat the giant in his life was a single stone and faith in God. This world tries to persuade us to conform to its way of thinking: fight for what you want, take control, and succeed at all cost. When all we really need is God to be our rock and to defeat whatever giant enemy we may be facing in our lives. Remember putting on the armor of God in Lesson 1, page 9?

True heroes persevere, not conform, when adversity comes.

Think about your favorite hero as you grew up. Your heroes probably changed with the wind. I know mine did. As a child, my parents were my heroes since they took care of all my problems. In my pre-teen years, famous people like the singing group The Go-Go's took their place. I know... I'm dating myself. As I moved into the teenage years, my hero became the teen idol, Leif Garrett. Well, okay, I'm not sure if he exemplified a hero or just a crush, but I had a picture of him on my wall, and I would daydream about him coming to my rescue on a white horse and falling madly in love with me!

Then in college my heroes became more scholarly, and I admired those that gave of themselves for our country or for a good cause. Now as I have matured, I find that I still admire individuals that give to a worthy cause or stand strong for a conviction. However, other than possibly Mother Theresa and a few of our US Presidents, I find that most of my heroes are not in the limelight, but rather ordinary people who overcame extraordinary circumstances, like David beating a giant with a stone.

ASK

Who has demonstrated heroism and had an impact on your life? Explain.

_____

_____

Hebrews 11, is known as the Heroes of Faith Chapter because of the great faith of each of these ordinary men and women who faced heartaches, adversity and sometimes tragedy; just like we do – and yet these individuals relied on

God despite their unpleasant and uncomfortable circumstances. In spite of it all, they persevered. Also, the object of their faith is critical. They totally relied on God. Here is an analogy: we get on an airplane and even though most of the time we do not see the pilot, we trust that the pilot has the necessary knowledge and skills to fly the plane. Faith is simply trusting (relying on) God to fly the plane. Trust is a discipline and the act of your will. We either believe or we doubt. Yes, Julia was overwhelmed and afraid at times, but then she just re-focused her mind on God and knew that He was right by her side every step of the way and cared about every detail of her life. She trusted Him even though she did not understand, and she persevered. She knew that Jesus was enough, **"…for I know whom I have believed and I am convinced that He is able to guard what I have entrusted to Him until the day of His return."** (**2 Timothy 1:12**) Even if weeping came in the night, Julia knew joy came in the morning, Psalm 30:5. Just as we go to the doctor for health problems, we must go to the Lord for heart problems. He is the only way we can hope to remain positive and persistent during difficult times.

Hebrews 11:1 (NLT) says, "Faith is the confidence that what we hope for will actually happen. It gives us assurance about things we cannot (yet) see."

Joy Comes in the Morning

Let's look at a few of these heroes:

> Hero of Faith, Noah. **"It was by faith that Noah built a large boat to save his family from the flood. He obeyed God, Who warned him about things that had never happened before."** (Hebrews 11:7 NLT)
>
> Imagine how Noah looked to everyone around him! Scholars tell us that the human race had never seen rain at that time in history. Noah claimed that God told him a great rain would come and flood the earth. I am pretty sure his neighbors and friends must have laughed at him and talked behind his back. They probably concluded he lost his mind and most likely criticized him for doing such a foolish thing as building a huge boat to house the local zoo population.
>
> A great enemy of the faith is criticism. When criticized for our faith, remember the heroes of faith who endured the same thing. Criticism can hold us back and keep us from reaching our full potential and doing good things for God. Stay optimistic and persevere through faith in order to accomplish great things for the Lord, like building an ark that ends up saving the entire human race.
>
> I imagine Noah feared his inability to accomplish such a huge task. I have been there at times too. Sometimes the task just seems overwhelming and I am faced with my own limitations and fear of failure. As I read the story of

Noah's ark, I am amazed at the detail from God. God did not say, "build and ark and let me know when you are done." He gave Noah specific instructions down to the most miniscule detail on how to build the boat, which tells me that God cares about every detail of our lives too. Noah accomplished his task despite his fears; all he had to do was listen and obey. He had to overcome the obstacles, such as, a lack of manpower, time, resources, and criticism from others, while continuing to provide for his family. Sound familiar? I have grown to love people who start a sentence with, "all you need to do is…" It is always easier said, than done. But, the key is, it can be done!

Just like Noah, I know that at times the burden of having cancer must have seemed too big and overwhelming for Julia. But God never left her alone. He always helped her to run the race set before her (Hebrews 12:1). Sometimes the thought of running that race can be exhausting. We tire of running our race, whatever that race may be, and want to cross the finish line, and move on to another race. Surely we could handle another race much easier. But this is our race. We don't get to choose the race, only how we run it.

I remember Julia, telling me that her husband was her true hero. He persevered through over seven years of chemotherapy, sickness, a bald head, pain, and unimaginable body reactions. Noah persevered as well. Bible experts say that the building of that ark of Noah's may have taken up to 100 years! That's what heroes do. They persevere.

Hero of Faith, Abraham. **"It was by faith that Abraham obeyed when God called him to leave home and go to another land that God would give him as his inheritance. He went without knowing where he was going. And even when he reached the land God promised him, he lived there by faith—for he was like a foreigner, living in tents." (Hebrews 11:8-9 NLT)**

Abraham, a highly respected and wealthy man, just picked up and left everything familiar because God told him to go. Can you imagine being told to leave your home, job, everything you know and have achieved, or acquired, and start walking? Furthermore, once Abraham reached his destination, he didn't receive the reward he thought he had been promised. He lived in a tent in the middle of nowhere, wondering what to do next. Even still, he trusted God one day at a time to fulfill His promise, by continually being obedient and waiting expectantly for a future reward. After learning she had cancer, Julia continued in obedience one day at a time, not sure where her journey would lead. It was like living in a tent in the middle of nowhere, wondering what to do next. But she trusted God and was determined to enjoy the journey along the way.

I reached a point in my life and career where I made a change, not knowing where it would lead. Most people would describe me at the time as a successful young professional. I earned a good salary, owned a sports car, a condo, and was able to travel with my friends all over the world. Then, I hit a point where I believed God asked me to leave it all, to let go of every crutch; my job, my title, my secure income, and my identity. I always said I would never leave a job without another one lined up. 'Never say never.' Do not misunderstand me. I do not believe following God means we have to give everything up and live as a missionary in Africa. That is a misconception that people have associated with being a "devout" Christian. However, I do believe there are times God might be nudging you to let go of something in order to receive something better. In my case, I appeared on the outside to have it all, but I was completely and utterly miserable at my job and in my life and decided God was definitely nudging me in another direction. I believed God could only change me if I changed my situation. I had no idea what would result from this decision other than going broke! However, I intentionally decided to trust, be obedient and wait expectantly on God. As I will tell you later, God worked amazing things in my life.

Hero of Faith, Sarah. **"It was by faith that even Sarah was able to have a child, though she was barren and was too old. She believed that God would keep his promise. And so a whole nation came from this one man who was as good as dead—a nation with so many people that, like the stars in the sky and the sand on the seashore, there is no way to count them." (Hebrews 11:11-12 NLT)**

We live in a society that says we should be married and have children by a certain age. Although waiting to get married certainly is more acceptable today, the reality remains that at some point nature will decide the child issue. That's where Sarah found herself. She was in her 80's and of course, not able to have children, but God had told her she would still have a son. At first she laughed. Maybe due to her age, she didn't believe God, or perhaps bitterness had set in after so many years. Where was God when she had desperately wanted a child in her younger years? This current announcement might have seemed like a cruel joke. Maybe she laughed out of joy and relief because God finally answered her prayers. Regardless, she came to understand that everything happens in God's timing.

Lesson Three: MY HERO

ASK

Which Hero of Faith can you relate to? Noah who was criticized, Abraham who left everything and relied completely on God, or Sarah who waited for her heart's desire? It can be a hero from Hebrews or another Biblical character you are familiar with. Why did you pick this person?

_____

_____

Waiting expectantly on God is where we recognize the miracles. I have heard it said that "when God closes one door, He opens another, but the hallway in between can be hell." The waiting and the persevering are tough, but they lead to growth, learning and the realization of our need for God. Maybe you are yearning for a baby, waiting for a mate, struggling to make your marriage work after so much hurt, praying for a promotion, striving to get out of debt, praying for healing that doesn't seem to come, or attempting to overcome an addiction which seems to make resisting temptation impossible. Know that with God all things are possible, and rest assured He will always give us a deeper relationship with Him because we learn to rely on Him in the waiting.

Joy Comes in the Morning

I continually learn this lesson in my own life. In particular, at 38 years old God finally blessed me with a life partner that eventually led to marriage. Trust me…that was not within my time-frame! I would have chosen to get married at least a *few* years earlier and start a family, but life took me another direction. I thought I would go nuts if one more person told me "it will happen when you least expect it." At 38 years old, I had expected it, not expected it, searched for it, ran from it, laughed about it, cried over it, and everything in between. I want IT and I want IT now! I was like a spoiled child stomping her feet and shaking her fist in the air saying, 'God, I have been faithful to You, unlike so many others, and I *deserve* someone special. Now, You owe me a really great guy. You promised! OK, I am just going out to find my own in the meantime!'

The truth is I wasn't doing such a good job of finding a great guy on my own. It felt like punishment, and as a single person, the sexual pressure was overwhelming. To be single and not sleeping around made me abnormal in this society, and Satan would grab hold of that thought and repeat it in my head until I worked myself into a frenzy. We are our own biggest enemy during difficult times in that we sometimes let our thought life and our emotions get the better of us. We believe we are victims of our emotions, that we are helpless to control them or how we feel, but Scripture is clear, that is simply not true. We control our thoughts and therefore our emotions.

"Finally, brothers, whatever is true, whatever is noble, whatever is right, whatever is pure, whatever is lovely, whatever is admirable—if anything is excellent or praiseworthy—think about such things. Whatever you have learned or received or heard from me, or seen in me—put it into practice. And the God of peace will be with you." (Philippians 4:8-9 NIV). I believe God wanted to give me His best, but I was too busy either being mad or informing Him what I wanted. I was not trusting God and allowing Him to bring that special person in my life. I would have missed Mr. Right if he walked up and told me God sent him!

God still had some work to do on my heart. I could have been bitter and resentful about having to wait so long. In all honesty, there were times when anger got the best of me, but I ultimately chose instead to trust in God's perfect timing for my life. I adopted the phrase, 'I would rather be single the rest of my life than married to the wrong man.' I often thought the phrase might somehow be prophetic and that I would remain single forever! I did not give up or resign myself to a life of loneliness though. I simply decided to wait expectantly and peacefully by trusting God's promise to fulfill the desire of my heart. After all it was a promise and I am convinced that God is not a liar. I remained faithful that He would either fulfill that promise or change my desire. Since my desire had not changed, I knew Mr. Right was out there and on his way to me. God, in His faithfulness and perfect timing, brought me a wonderful man. He did it during those months after I quit my demanding job, was unemployed, and wondering what God would do with me next.

Sarah could have resented God for not blessing her with a child earlier, but instead she experienced a miracle. Julia could have resented God for not healing her body when she got sick or for not being able to have a child, and for the unbelievable emotional and physical pain. Instead, she chose to wait on God and cling to Him, **"For just as the heavens are higher than the earth, so are my ways higher than your ways and my thoughts higher than your thoughts."** **(Isaiah 55:9)** She experienced the miracle of life one day at a time. Julia realized that she was the miracle! She is a true hero.

There are several more Heroes mentioned in Hebrews 11. You can probably name some heroes of your own. I have several heroes in my life that come to mind. One is my step-mom who had a mastectomy. Several years after that, she had lung cancer and then melanoma of the lymph nodes…twice. She has been cut into so many times; the doctor said her body looks like a road map.

Despite everything, she has one of the best attitudes I have ever run across. She had more energy on her interferon shots than most healthy people have on a normal day. I remember asking her how she went through all of that pain and kept her spirits up. She replied, "You do what you have to, and you have to fight whatever it is, and then take one day at a time." She believes a positive attitude and faith are the reasons she survived. **Hebrews 11:34 says, "faith makes weak men strong."** Faith gave her the strength to persevere. She never gave up. Ever.

Another hero of mine is my friend, Dawn, who is now a pastor. She cares more for others than her own comfort, she makes me laugh, she has a great attitude, and inspires me to be the same. She is often my reality check and the person who holds me accountable. She would love to be married and have a family of her own eventually. We had many conversations to the effect of, "hurry up God, what are you waiting for. I am not getting any younger here…" But despite our kidding, pleading, and crying at times, we both know that God has a plan for her life as well as mine. He already has plans for prosperity and hope. He knows the desires of our hearts before we know and promises to fulfill them…in His timing, not ours. She has been my friend through the good times when we are laughing so hard we have tears rolling down our cheeks and through the bad times when we were whining and complaining. She gives of her time and never expects anything in return. I always pray that I can be half the friend to her that she is to me.

Of course, Julia is also one of my heroes and the inspiration for this book. At only 32 years old she found out she had a rare cancer. She chose to dance through life, despite her "dread disease." She went through so much pain internally and yet she showed herself to be the most encouraging, upbeat person I have ever met. People ask me all of the time how she maintained such a great attitude. I tell them, 'She had a great attitude before she got cancer and her positive attitude just magnified through her struggles.' She would tell you the Lord carried her through. She made life fun by sharing her faith, encouraging others, and living each day to the fullest; just persevering and waiting on God. She lived **Hebrews 10:23-25 (NLT), which says, "Let us hold tightly without wavering to the hope we affirm, for God can be trusted to keep His promise. Let us think of ways to motivate each other to acts of love and good works.**

Lesson Three: MY HERO

**And let us not neglect our meeting together, as some
people do, but encourage one another, especially now that
the day of His return is drawing near."**

Most of all, Jesus is my hero! Without Him, where
would I be? Where would I turn when faced with adversity?
Would I hide from my problems and fill the void with
workaholism, sex, drugs and alcohol, gambling or worse?
Without Jesus being willing to die on the cross for me, where
would I be? He completes me.

ASK

Who are your heroes that set an example for
you to follow?

_____

_____

ASK

Who or what is your giant? Do you believe
God will help you defeat your giant?

_____

_____

ASK

How can you be a Hero of Faith to someone else this week? Write that person's name and your plan of action.

_____

_____

Lesson Four: WEAR WORN OUT BLUE JEANS

"Yet those who wait for the Lord will gain new strength..."
Isaiah 40:31

For years Julia and I enjoyed monthly shopping sprees together. Julia liked to shop at boutiques. She had exquisite taste in clothes and took pleasure in finding unique articles of clothing to add to her wardrobe. While the shopping days and time spent with Julia were always interesting, the boutiques could get a little pricey. For instance, $200 blue jeans, with holes! We both giggled and reminisced at how we use to run out and spend $19.95 on a pair of blue jeans, throw them in the wash with bleach to get the faded look, and wear those jeans until they were frayed at the bottom and had holes in them. That was the style back then too and it was "cool." We paid $20 for a pair of jeans and got a $200 look without knowing it! The difference was ours didn't have a designer label of course, and it took time to wear them out and get them just right. In this day of instant gratification, we do not want to wait for our jeans to wear out. We prefer to take the easy way and simply pay to get the look we want right now, no matter what the cost.

Joy Comes in the Morning

Isn't that just like life? The days of paying our dues through hard work, perseverance, and waiting for things we yearn for in life have been reduced to just pay for it now, or more likely later with credit! We buy the latest-greatest, only to discover two months later, there is a new latest-greatest and the cycle continues. We are never satisfied. For some unexplained reason it seems only through delayed gratification, where we have waited and persevered through hard work, that we seem to find real satisfaction. Don't we often feel we need that new outfit *now* regardless of whether we can afford it now or not? Sometimes we appreciate things more when we have to wait to obtain. It's not always material things either. What about a goal? If we could reach our goals tomorrow, would we truly be satisfied if they were so easily attainable? If it were that easy, don't you think everyone would be achieving the same goal? Where is the satisfaction in that? Looking back at our lives, imagine what we would have missed if we did not persevere every time we fell down and then had the strength to get up and try again! No one likes to fall down, but we all do at times. It is that in between time where we can demonstrate the courage to pull ourselves up again, strive to maintain hope, and have the strength to persevere while we are down, and the prayers to

Lesson Four: WEAR WORN OUT BLUE JEANS

keep moving forward that leads us to finding contentment and peace.

ASK   Describe a time you lost hope and fell down. What was the turning point that made you pull yourself up and try again?

_____

_____

In other words, we should take pride in wearing out our jeans the old fashioned way; tattered, torn, and worn from pulling ourselves up time and time again.

I literally have a pair of old jeans with broken belt loops. Sometimes the jeans needed a little extra effort to pull them up over my hips--hips that I am convinced are hereditary. I can't seem to throw out these jeans because they are extremely comfortable and I've worn them in just right. Therefore, I did what anyone would do; grabbed the belt loops and yanked those jeans up until they were perfectly in place on me. I was not going to be defeated by blue jeans and big hips. That's a true story, but I find the analogy ironic. Sometimes it does take an extra effort to pull ourselves up. When we fall, our minds are filled with doubt and fear that paralyzes us. We might get up half way and then an obstacle arises and BAM, we fall back down.

Joy Comes in the Morning

Several years after leaving the hotel industry, I decided to start my own business. Anyone who has started a business will tell you, there are many obstacles that get in the way. I thought it would be easy. Of course expenses were higher than anticipated and BAM, I fell down and wanted to quit. Sales were taking longer than planned, and BAM, I wanted to quit again. My husband got frustrated with the timeline. I felt inadequate until it caused tension and BAM, I almost quit. BAM, BAM, BAM! I fell down until the back side of my jeans were faded and worn from falling on my "derriere" time after time. I fell so many times until the belt loops were literally broken from pulling myself up over and over and over again. I fell down and pulled myself up, I was not going to be defeated by negative thoughts and a setback or two. I fell down and I pulled myself up even when my doubts and my fears threatened to paralyze me.

My friend, Julia, pulled herself up every day by the belt loops. She was just 32 years old when she was told she had cancer and only six months to live. Some of you remember seeing the movie, "The Bucket List." What a fantastic movie! Julia had her own bucket list prior to the release of the movie. She called it her "wish list." She had always written down her goals and dreams of places to go, adventures to enjoy…until she found out she had stage 4 incurable cancer. What was the point in continuing the list? The truth is she desperately needed her wish list to give her a reason to get up in the morning versus just waiting to expire. So she began to write her list of life wishes in attainable detail. That year she went to Italy, check, swam with the dolphins, check, volunteered at the raptor center, check, check, check, and started listing more life wishes on a new sheet paper. I believe the hope of reaching those goals, plus actually meeting some, gave her a positive attitude and the strength to grab her belt loops, pull herself up, and keep on going for another seven years.

I have fallen down many, many times through the years and God's love always gave me hope and purpose to get up again. God even speaks to us through His Word when He promises, **"...I will never desert you, nor will I ever forsake you, so that we confidently say, the Lord is my Helper, I will not be afraid. What shall man do to me?" (Hebrews 13:5-6)** We have all heard and made fun of the saying, "I've fallen and I can't get up." I say, grab hold of your belt loops and pull yourself up again!

May we take pride in wearing jeans the old fashioned way: patches on the pockets because we've been carrying God's Word everywhere we venture. Julia pulled herself up every day and did the best she could with the day God gave her. She carried God's Word with her daily to give her strength and purpose. She had so many patches; her jeans looked like a quilt. Well, not literally, but she turned to the Word of God to give her strength, to keep her focused and to gain wisdom. I asked her on several occasions what kept her going and she always responded, God. Reading His Words gave her peace, comfort and energy each day. Admittedly some days were easier than others but she never blamed God for her situation, she trusted His plan was bigger than she could imagine.

There is nothing stronger than the Word of God. Not advice from well-meaning friends and family, not the words of a counselor and not even our own stubborn determination. God's Word is our amour that protects us during life's battle. We don't know the devil is lying to us if we don't know the Word of God. When Jesus was led into the desert for 40 days, He repeated God's Word to give Him strength. **"Then Jesus was led by the Spirit into the wilderness to be tempted by the devil." (Matthew 4:1) Jesus answered in verse 4, "It is written: 'Man does not live on bread alone, but on every word that proceeds out of the mouth of God'." Jesus answered him in verse 7, "It is also written: 'Do not put the Lord your God to the test'." Jesus said to him in verse 10, "Away from me, Satan! For it is written:**

Lesson Four: WEAR WORN OUT BLUE JEANS

**'Worship the Lord your God, and serve him only'."
Finally in verse 11, "Then the devil left him, and angels
came and began to minister to Him."** First Jesus quoted
Scripture and then the angels came and helped Him. If Jesus
quoted Scripture to receive God's strength, then it stands to
reason we can overcome adversity through abiding in God's
strength too. Yet, we often try by using our own might.
Have you ever felt attacked in your job or in a relationship,
or in life, and there seems to be no way out? That is exactly
where Satan wants us...doubting and ineffective. I know
when I went through a particular rough patch in my life, the
"what if" thoughts controlled my mind. I had to battle them
daily with memorizing Scripture and at times saying it out
loud. There is power in quoting Scripture. There is not
power in talking to all of my friends about my struggles.
Yet, so often, that is the first place I turn. I have challenged
myself to begin to memorize Scripture so when challenges
arise, I stop, pray, and repeat those verses out loud. Then I
continue my day with a belief that things will work out.
With a combination of Scripture and prayer, things always
work out according to His plan.

May we take pride in wearing our jeans the old
fashioned way; the knees on our jeans have holes from
falling on them in prayer. Once we know Scripture, praying

God's Word on our knees holds power beyond
comprehension. **Hebrews 4:12 says, "For the word of God
is living and active. Sharper than any double-edged
sword, it penetrates even to dividing soul and spirit, joints
and marrow; it judges the thoughts and attitudes of the
heart."** Speaker and author Joyce Meyers says, "Think less
and thank more," and I believe that little sentence is so
powerful. We can think our way into a bad mood before we
even get out of bed in the morning. Or we can pray our way
into a good mood. Prayer is a spiritual weapon. I have been
learning the power of prayer on my knees. Not literally
always on my knees, sometimes I am jogging on the
treadmill at the gym and saying my prayers. I am so focused
that one time a friend came up to speak to me and when I
turned my head to speak, I lost my balance and flew off the
treadmill. It was like watching a television sitcom! Talking
to the Lord through prayer can be done so many ways. An
easy acronym for a model of prayer that I follow is ACTS; A:
Adoration, praise to God for who He is, C: Confession of our
sins, T: Thanksgiving for all of our blessings, and S:
Supplication, or making our requests to God. Adoration,
Confession, Thanksgiving, Supplication. Adoration through
song or thankfulness that God cares for me tends to lift my
heart with the realization that I matter to the God of this

universe. The more I praise God, the smaller my problems seem to appear. Confession is not because God doesn't already know my sins but so that I am humbled and realize that I will never be good enough without the Lord in my life. Thankfulness for my family and friends and all the blessings the Lord has bestowed upon me by His grace and not because of anything I have done to earn them. Thanking the Lord even for difficulties that help me to grow as a person. Finally, Supplication, praying and asking God for help for my family, friends and myself because He cares for every concern I have.

Stop now & say a prayer according to ACTS.

So, may we take pride in wearing our jeans the old fashioned way; faded from persevering through many washes and wears. After 15 years in sales in the hotel industry, I left my job. There were times during the next year without a steady income, without a title on my business cards, without all of my crutches in life, where I did not know if I could get up again. But I persevered and kept job hunting and watching those pennies. There were also times as a single person that dating and being disappointed yet again, seemed too much to bear. Then, within a year after leaving my job, I met my husband while attending a meeting, ironically, in the lobby of the hotel where I had previously worked. God has a sense of humor! Then, two days after we got engaged, I started my dream job. Yes, I fell down, yes I persevered through the tough times, and yes I had the courage to grab hold of my belt loops and pull myself up again.

Julia persevered against all odds and lived a vibrant productive life for another seven years. She persevered when she was down and did not want to get up again. The days the pain attempted to keep her down, she grabbed her belt loops and pulled until they broke if necessary. When I probably would have felt sorry for myself, she went after things on her wish list and made memories with those she loved. She went out and helped others to keep from focusing on her own health. The times she was in the hospital, she flashed the doctors a half moon from the hospital gown. Other times she would theatrically ask if they wanted to take her blood, as if she were a vampire. She persevered through what she referred to as her dance in life.

Which leads me to add; take pride in wearing jeans the old fashioned way with the bottoms of our jeans frayed from walking (or dancing) through the journey of life.

Along the way make sure we are ministering to others in actions and words. **"Live a life filled with love for**

others, following the example of Christ, who loved you
and gave Himself as a sacrifice to take away your sins."
(Ephesians 5:2 NIV) "Dear friends, let us continue to
love one another, for love comes from God. Anyone who
loves is a child of God and knows God." (1 John 4:7 NLT)

So I say, the next time we shop for a pair of blue
jeans, be determined to wear them until they are faded,
tattered, worn, torn, and ripped. May they always remind us
of our strength to pull ourselves up by the belt loops when we
fall; carrying the Word of God and the prayers that sustained
us and gave us hope. May they also remind us of our
perseverance through difficult times, and may they be frayed
from a journey worth walking throughout the dance of our
life!

ACT

Share or write your journey that brought you to
the Lord and made you grow. It doesn't have to be long but
it is important to know how to verbalize and share your story
with others.

If you don't have a story, pray that God will come into your
life and give you a story to share with others. It does not

have to be dramatic; it can simply be your unique story. God
uses all journeys to lead other to him.

_____

_____

_____

_____

_____

_____

_____

_____

Lesson Five: *QUIET CONVERSATIONS*

"A word aptly spoken is like apples of gold in settings of silver."
Proverbs 25:11

I snuck a card in my husband's luggage that said, "When you're not here I tend to talk to myself. I'm interesting and I make some good points, but I'm no substitute for you." We have been raised in a society that likes noise. We like talking to ourselves or other people constantly, listening to loud music, a television on at all times, long telephone conversations, or video games, and the list goes on. There is, of course, a time for noise and talking to others and that fellowship is important. However, what we really need and so rarely receive is quiet conversations. We all need some quiet time to talk to God, and yes, to talk to ourselves. I know it sounds silly but we all need to give ourselves a pep talk on a regular basis. We need to fill our minds with positive images and thoughts; otherwise, the negative has a way of sneaking into the recesses of our mind and wreaking havoc.

My pastor, Dr. David Chadwick, has said there are three types of conversations you can have: (1) conversations with God, (2) conversations with ourselves, and (3) conversations with other people.

Conversations with God are the most important, whether you are the one going through the suffering or the one standing by that person's side and holding their hand. Pray, pray and pray some more while pouring out your whole heart and soul. Thank God for the time we have, the blessings in our life, and ask for healing, and be still. **"Always be joyful. Never stop praying. Be thankful in all circumstances, for this is God's will for you who belong to Christ Jesus." (1Thessalonians 5:17 NLT) "Be still, and know that I am God" (Psalm 46:10 NIV).** It has taken me years to learn this, but I have finally learned in life to go to God first with my requests and then be still and let Him speak to me. Then I seek out just one or two individuals whom I trust to share my deepest thoughts. I've learned to listen to God first and the selected friends second. There were many times I did this backwards, I called my friends first so that I could whine about my life and then I would say a quick prayer. The first conversation we have, above all others, should be with our Lord and Savior, Jesus Christ.

Pray in small groups of two or three, or by yourself, for an area or problem in your life that you need some help in right now. It is okay to ask for help from God and others.

Conversations with ourselves can deflate or uplift us in a heartbeat. I can depress myself with my negative self talk faster than you can snap your fingers. That internal voice says things like, "This isn't fair… Boy, I messed up bad …I should have done this or that…No one loves me…What's wrong with me…If God loved me, He would fix this or heal me or heal my loved one, my marriage, my work relationships…." Stop the negative thought patterns and learn positive self-talk. We can decide to avoid negative thoughts but, unless replaced with something positive, the negative thoughts will creep back in our mind. Even Jesus had to quote His Father (Scripture) to remain strong when being tempted in the wilderness by Satan. Jesus prayed at Gethsemane for the "cup to be taken from him." He did not want to go through the pain of separation from God. But He also prayed that the Father's Will be done. If Jesus had to pray and fill His mind with God's Word, how much more do we need to do these things? Pull out Scripture and read daily. God will give us a particular Scripture that will start healing our soul. I like to write my favorite verses on note cards and pull them out when I need a "Jesus fix." Half the battle is simply not letting my mind wander down negative paths. **"Watch over your heart with all diligence, for from it flows the springs of life."** (Proverbs 4:23) **"For as he thinks within himself, so he is."** (Proverbs 23:7) I know controlling self-talk is not easy. Remember, when battling our own thoughts, it is a war in our minds and most battles are not simple. Every day we have to take our thoughts captive. Just when we think we have mastered our emotions, they trick us into negativity again. *We* control our own emotions, not the other way around. We do not have to live a defeated life. We are already victorious in Christ.

Memorize one verse that is encouraging to you and say it out loud for the group or to yourself in a mirror.

The third type of conversation, conversations with others, can be encouraging or discouraging as well. We all have friends that drain us emotionally just by being around them. They can be so needy because they talk non-stop about themselves and their problems. They rarely ask or even care about anyone else's life. Do not spend much time around these types of people, and perhaps more importantly, do not be or become one of those negative, self-centered people. We can help those that struggle, but some

Lesson Five: QUIET CONVERSATIONS

individuals like a captive ear to hear them complain about how they are the victims. These individuals have no intention of trying to find a healthy resolution. We can give advice and encouragement until we have none left to give and they still do not hear. These are the friends who actually like all of that drama in their lives. Give an encouraging word and then move on. Never forget the power of words. **"Pleasant words are a honeycomb, sweet to the soul and healing to the bones." (Proverbs 16:24) "Anxiety in a man's heart weighs it down, but a good word makes it glad." (Proverbs 12:25)** Also, make sure to identify positive people that are trustworthy to call on during difficult times when a word of encouragement is needed. Do not seek out people that will "fuel the fire" for anger. That is like trying to find someone that will help justify the way we are feeling. Rather, find friends that are honest even if it hurts our feelings. That will be a reality check and give us the encouragement we *need* versus the encouragement we *want*.

One day while Julia's pastor visited her in the hospital, a nearby patient overheard and made a comment to them. Julia and her pastor spent the next several hours encouraging this woman whom neither of them knew. The poor woman had been abused by her husband to the point of being hospitalized and now she was afraid to leave him. She desperately needed that conversation and encouragement. Had Julia and her pastor not been open to helping her, who knows what might have happened?

Sometimes just sharing our personal story of adversity with others and being genuine is all they need. Often people feel their own problems are worse than anyone else's. That's why Julia gave her testimony whenever she was asked. She believed that if even one person felt encouraged or gained hope through their difficulties because of her illness, she was serving God. The only way she could provide encouragement to others was by being prepared through talks with God and with herself each and every day.

ASK   What is one thing you can do to make yourself available to someone else in need, whether they have asked for help or not? Write down one encouraging thing you can say to that person today.

_____

_____

Before going to the next lesson, let me take a moment to address the families and friends of someone who may be suffering. I was out of town on business several years ago. God in His infinite wisdom and mercy knew I would need someone by my side that night and it just so happened that I was out of town with another person from the company. I usually went out of town by myself, but this particular client required two of us giving simultaneous presentations. It also just so happened that the person I was traveling with had gone through an experience very similar to my own five years earlier. So when I got the telephone call that my step-mom had lung cancer, she immediately called her father who had also been diagnosed with lung cancer and let me talk with him. It gave me such a peace to be able to ask questions of someone who had survived lung cancer. The future was not quite as scary to face, and his story helped me have a much brighter outlook as I went to the hospital the next day to be with my step-mom during surgery. You may believe that this was a coincidence; however, I believe that it was divine intervention.

I also remember five years later again being told that my step-mom had melanoma of the lymph nodes. I would walk in the door of my home after work and fall to my knees crying. I was still single at the time and home alone in the evenings. The aloneness was almost overwhelming and the frustration with not knowing the outcome of her cancer seemed unbearable. Friends stayed away during that time because they didn't know what to say to me, or they assumed that I was doing okay and did not need them. After all, I was usually the one my friends called for support when they were dealing with problems, not typically the one needing support.

I remember thinking that I would love someone to stop by with a movie and popcorn and just sit with me. When I mentioned this to my friends later, that I had felt so alone during that time, they said that they did not realize I needed them. I was forced to take ownership of the fact that I had never asked for their help. I just assumed they should know. Guess what? People can't read our mind. We need to be able to reach out and call a friend just to be by our side or let us cry on their shoulder. That's what friends are for. They just don't want to be "in the way", but friends will understand if we tell them we need alone time too. Remember, we were never meant to handle life's challenges on our own. We are meant for relationship with God and with other people.

I had a trip to Europe planned during the second round of my step-mom's melanoma treatments and I was determined to cancel, but she insisted I take the trip anyway. She reminded me the treatments would involve a long process lasting almost two years, and I couldn't just sit and stare at her for all of that time. So I went to Europe. That's when I finally got my peace. I would sit on the side of a mountain in Scotland and look at the beauty all around me

Lesson Five: QUIET CONVERSATIONS

that God created and I would pray. I would just sit and let God refresh me and give me peace. Then I would only allow positive thoughts in my mind.

It ended up being a great trip and when I came back I was able to go to the hospital to visit my step-mom. I would sit and read encouraging books to her during her tests and hold her hand as she was coming out of surgery. I was able to tell her confidently that God was in control, no matter what. All of this is to say, we must make sure to take care of ourselves too and get our emotional encouragement during times of trying to comfort others.

ASK   What is something you do to re-energize and stay strong in your faith during times of a loved one's struggle?

_____

_____

Lesson Six: DRIVE-BY PLANTINGS

"Each of you should look not only to your own interests,
but also to the interests of others."
Philippians 2:4

Shortly after my husband and I started dating, he
suggested taking me to a dinner buffet, to which I responded,
"If I wanted to serve myself, I would cook it myself at
home." Although this wasn't quite true because I never
cooked! My idea of cooking was heating food up in the
microwave. For years I worked in the hotel industry and I
made sure I became friends with the chefs and showed them
much respect. If you have ever worked with a chef, you
know that they take tremendous pride in their creations and
genuinely enjoy sharing their talents with others. Since I
fully enjoyed their talents too, I figured it was a win-win.
Every family holiday or event where I was required to take a
covered dish, I gave the chef opportunity to explore his
creative side again. This proves the theory, "It's not what
you know, but who you know that matters." (Ironically
enough, this is a good quote about knowing Jesus too).

In addition to not being able to boil water, I did not
enjoy cleaning the house and certainly did not have a green

thumb. So my future husband was beginning to think I was "high maintenance." Lucky for me, he was willing to take the risk and married me anyway. Lo and behold, I have learned to cook, I still don't enjoy cleaning the house, and with a little advice from my mother-in-law, I now have 24 plants in my house that are still alive! In other words, there are things in life we can improve on, if we are willing to step out of our comfort zone. We might even come to enjoy things we never thought we would like. With a little faith, love, and hope we can accomplish great things...maybe even a "drive-by planting"...keep reading.

It started one day when Julia mistakenly received a phone call from creditors meant for her neighbor, who was going through a bitter divorce. Julia walked over to tell her neighbor about the phone call. As she walked up onto the porch, "it looked like spooky Halloween," with spider webs, dead flowerbeds, and peeling door paint. The condition of the porch broke her heart. Later that evening, Julia returned with her mother, both of them wearing black sweats and t-shirts, and in the shadows of the night-- bypassing motion lights and dogs-- anonymously swept the porch and planted new flowers in the neighbor's flowerbeds. Of course the woman never knew who had given of their time and effort for her, but several days later as Julia was driving down the street, she noticed a huge sign in the woman's front yard with the words "THANK YOU". Just a simple act of kindness done anonymously under the cover of night, and yet it brought a smile to a grieving woman's face. Julia had given faith, love, and hope to someone in need.

First, we all need faith. God is not a genie in a bottle that grants us three wishes. He is our Father, Provider, Comforter, Caregiver, and Friend. So when I talk about a faith that surpasses all understanding, I am not talking about going to church on Sundays and calling yourself a Christian. I like to repeat the saying that "sitting in church doesn't make you a Christian any more than sitting in the garage makes you a car." Being Christian is so much more. I am talking about having a relationship with God like we do with any person that we love, depend on and lean on.

Think of a relationship in which you feel able to share your deepest secrets and know the person will love you anyway. Think of a relationship where you want to do things for the other person to make them happy, and not because you "have to." Think of a relationship where the other person wants to do things for you too because they enjoy seeing you happy. We all yearn for that kind of relationship and yet so few seem to obtain it, which makes me wonder if God wants us to fill that yearning with His love alone. I believe God gives us glimpses of His love through our relationships with others, but other people cannot complete us. Is God enough in our life? In other words, is God enough when our marriage is failing, or does our identity depend on the approval of our spouse? Is God enough when we lose our job, or is our identity wrapped up in how much money we make and the title on our business cards? You get the point. A fulfilling relationship with God leads to a deep-rooted faith that is hard to even put into words. But when the tough times come, and they will, we experience a peace greater than our human capacity to grasp.

It all starts with just asking God to come into our life and provide wisdom. We don't read a book about someone before we decide to get to know them, do we? We just initially decide we want to get to know a person by spending time with them going to dinners, movies, walks, and talking. The more time we spend with a person we begin to see their true character, and perhaps eventually come to trust and love them. The same is true with the Lord. We do not have to read the entire Bible and have all the answers. The requirement only consists of a desire to get to know Him and then ask Him to come into our life. Then we spend time with the Lord through reading Scripture, going to church, talking to others, and praying. The more time we spend with God, the more we will get to know Him, see His character, and see that He is good and true. Then I guarantee you will fall in love with our awesome Savior. As Julia said in one of her speeches, "My priorities in order are; God, family, others, and then self – show grace to all. God wants a relationship with you not just for you to believe in Him, but to have a real relationship with him. Even the devil believes in God.--. Spend time, talk to Him (pray), read His word, talk with other believers. Religion isn't just a crutch; it's a life support. If you take action now and have a good foundation, you'll be prepared when adversity happens."

God came to earth in human flesh and experienced every emotion and temptation we have or ever will experience (which makes Him a personal God). He died on a cross for our sins (which makes Him a merciful, forgiving God), and He rose again three days later and ascended into heaven (which makes him an awesome God). God says to believe in Christ and that we are a sinner in need of a Savior. We all sin in varying degrees, and God doesn't measure by degrees. As the Scriptures say, **"There is none righteous, not even one…For all have sinned and fall short of the glory of God." (Romans 3:10 & 23 NIV)** Let Christ come into your life and take your burdens from you. You will experience an inner peace and a rest like you never have before. Read the following verses and message taken from the New Living Translation, Tyndale House Publishers, Inc. (with a few of the points paraphrased):

John 3: 27 – "John replied, God in heaven appoints each person's work." God has a plan for our life. To know that plan, we must first know God.

John 8:12 – "Jesus said to the people, 'I am the light of the world. If you follow me, you won't be stumbling through the darkness, because you will have the light that leads to life'." God's plan promises to give us life everlasting by giving us direction through trusting Him and His guidance.

John 14:27 – "I am leaving you with a gift - peace of mind and heart. And the peace I give isn't like the peace the world gives. So don't be troubled or afraid." God's plan brings the gift of peace so we won't be afraid and can endure hardships as they come.

John 3:16 – "For God so loved the world that He gave His only Son, so that everyone who believes in Him will not perish but have eternal life." God's plan is for us to live with Him in heaven for eternity.

Colossians 1:22 – "Yet now He has brought you back as His friends. He has done this through His death on the cross in His own human body. As a result, He has brought you into the very presence of God, and we are holy and blameless as we stand before Him without a single fault." Recognize that Jesus died on that cross just for you and me, to be the ultimate sacrifice. When we ask Him to forgive our sins, He will not see our faults any more.

ASK

Do you believe God is enough in your current situation? Why or why not?

_____

_____

As I mentioned, first we need faith. Believing in Christ is faith. Second, we need to love others. It is difficult to be depressed about self-issues when focused on other people. We live in a society in which the typical person only cares about his or her circle of friends. We ignore the person next to us on the airplane so we do not have to listen to their problems for the next several hours. We avoid getting involved in Bible Study groups because it is just one more time commitment that causes guilt if we miss a meeting. Keeping up with the friends we have is challenging enough, so we avoid making new friends. Sometimes it just seems like an effort to spend time with the people we know, much less a complete stranger. Basically we have become very selfish with our time because we seem to have so little of it. Yet, we are here for a purpose and it is not to isolate ourselves, accumulate as many toys as we can or to outperform the next guy. Our purpose is not to find hobbies and careers that occupy all of our time so that we have an excuse to avoid true intimacy with other people. Jesus is all about relationships with other people. So I would venture to say, God's plan for us involves loving other people and reaching out to people that are in need.

Julia did this well. She had a gift of making someone feel that they were the only person that mattered. She asked questions about their life and showed a genuine interest and concern. She believed her purpose was to help others. She truly believed that was why God allowed her cancer diagnosis, so that she could help and encourage others that were going through an illness. She also believed focusing on other people kept her from feeling sorry for herself and her circumstances. She believed, as I have heard Christian author and speaker Joyce Meyers say, that even though she had a *reason* to feel sorry for herself, she did not have the *right*. God tells us to be joyful despite our circumstances. It is easy to have joy when life is coasting along without any difficulties, but not so much when huge

Lesson Six: *DRIVE-BY PLANTINGS*

problems develop. Julia lived by, **"Do nothing from selfishness or empty conceit, but with humility of mind, let each of you regard one another as more important than himself; do not merely look out for your own personal interests, but also for the interests of others."** **(Philippians 2:3-4)** Julia would say, "You don't have to go to Africa to help other people, you can be a missionary in your own backyard." That belief led her to what she referred to as "drive-by plantings." After that evening planting flowers for her neighbor, she would continue to plant flowers for people that were hurting as a way to bring a smile to them. Once when she was in the hospital, Julia's friends brought her a huge, fake sunflower with a big smiley face in the middle. Julia laughed out loud. Then she realized that many of the hospital patients could not have real flowers in their rooms due to hospital rules and sensitivities to certain scents. She made it her mission to buy every artificial sunflower she could find and personally delivered them…yes, in her hospital gown. She brought a little sunshine to others, and on occasion, even a "moon" or two. You know how those hospital gowns have a mind of their own sometimes!

She also joined Junior League to participate in their volunteer activities in the community. She gave her testimony at churches or support groups, and did one-on-one counseling to cancer patients when asked. She volunteered at the Natural Science Center, planned vacations for her family, set aside quality time with her husband and her friends. Julia kept her mind busy from wallowing in her problems and she chose to live every day to the fullest as if each day was a precious gift from God. And it was, especially since she already discovered that every day starts with the light of life and that joy comes in the morning.

We have heard many times that we should live our lives as if every day were our last, but so few of us actually do. Or maybe we do live each day as if it were our last and regretfully most of us would be depressed and complaining on our last day on earth. We need to learn to enjoy the beauty and the people around us. Enjoy God's creation of which we are a part. As I spent more time with Julia, I found new enjoyment in simple things like taking a walk, getting my nails done, or just running errands. Julia never lost her childlike wonder and playfulness. Julia helped me to see things with new eyes, even in the mundane tasks. Julia would get so excited about grocery shopping; just to check out the cheese sample of the day was like she was tasting cheese for the first time. When was the last time you got excited about going to the grocery store?

Lesson Six: DRIVE-BY PLANTINGS

She gave great advice, love, support, and encouragement to me, in addition to so many others. Sometimes I thought, "How did she do that to me again? I came to encourage her and somehow she managed to encourage me." My problems probably seemed so insignificant compared to what she endured on a daily basis, and yet she acted like my silly dilemma of the day was the most important thing in the world to her. Julia knew the true meaning of love.

ASK   What is a charity or activity for others that you will get involved with, or are currently involved in, to keep your focus off yourself and your problems? Challenge yourself to find new enjoyment in a simple task using childlike wonder.

_____

_____

_____

_____

_____

_____

Joy Comes in the Morning

Finally, hope when all seems lost. This comes from knowing the Lord, from a support group of friends or family members, and from giving encouragement back to others. **"A joyful heart is good medicine, but a broken spirit dries up the bones." (Proverbs 17:22)** Most of us can be so stubborn! We believe we can handle things on our own. That is called pride. We all need humility at times and we need support from others. **"If two of you agree down here on earth concerning anything you ask, My Father in heaven will do it for you." (Matthew 18:19 NLT) "So encourage each other and build each other up, just as you are already doing." (1 Thessalonians 5:11 NLT)** We need to allow people to give us support and accept their support graciously.

Most of us feel so helpless when those we care about are suffering because we can't take the pain away. Julia's strength and fun-loving attitude caused me to forget that she had cancer. But sometimes she would pick the phone up and call me to say that she needed a "Sherri fix." That became her way of asking for encouragement.

Julia always reminded me of the time I drove to Greensboro after one of her chemotherapy treatments. I walked in and took one look at her pale face, observed the snail pace of her steps, and knew the pain she worked hard to hide. I sent her to bed immediately. She slept while I sat in the living room filtering the constant stream of phone calls. Since eating had been a challenge and she had lost so much weight, I prepared cottage cheese and pears for her when she woke up. It was high protein and easy for her to eat. From that moment on, that combination became her comfort food. There are many ways to give encouragement; words, acts of kindness such as making meals, cleaning the house or running errands for others, or simply sitting and watching a movie together and not saying a word.

I have come to realize the importance of encouraging others not only when someone is physically sick, but also on a daily basis to those in your family, those you work with, and even strangers you meet on an airplane.

One time when Julia was in the ICU (intensive care unit) due to salmonella poisoning, the doctors thought she might not survive. Her body could not fight the infection because her resistance was down from the recent chemotherapy. Most of her family flew in that night. One family member gave her a basket when she woke up filled with travel books and pictures of Greece, with a note that said, "Julia, you have to get better quickly so we can go to Greece." Julia had always wanted to travel to Greece. The basket was just what the doctor ordered for Julia; hope and something to look forward to.

Sometimes we need to receive encouragement and other times we need to give encouragement. That is the cycle of good friendships. **"A friend is always loyal, and a brother is born to help in time of need." (Proverbs 17:17 NLT)** This was exactly what Julia received from her brother. (following is an excerpt from Julia's speech on adversity)

I have experience in 2 things: The engineering technology of a variable drive speed motor in an air compressor OR how to overcome adversity. I have chosen to talk to you for the next several hours on air compressors! (tee hee)

All right, let's talk about overcoming adversity, which are blessings in disguise, and a positive attitude.

I just had surgery in April; rotor-rootered my lung. Afterward for a couple months – going up stairs became a breathing chore. Even before that, the salmonella that filled my left lung prevented me from yoga and other exercise, so I didn't do … anything. To give you some background – our family decided to go to Tucson to celebrate my dad's 70th birthday – at the same time, there was a big bike race, 4, 35, 50, 75, and 100 - mile bike race. Our family said lets all do the 4-mile together, but my dad's going for the 35 and my brother is training for the 100. Last weekend I visited my brother for his birthday and he asked me about the race. I said – 'I can hardly do stairs; I couldn't do even the 4 miler. I'll just cheer you on.' A day went by and we opened up his birthday gifts and he said had one for me. 'Hmmm, what's this for?' He grinned, he loves getting someone the perfect gift. I opened it and it's a Lance Armstrong yellow bike jersey. Embroidered with my name; Tour de Tucson, Team Captain. On the back, my favorite bible verses and of all my family members names under the headline in big white letters; 'Backing you up!' 'What does this mean?' I asked. "Let's go for a walk," he said, "and put on the yellow jersey." So, I did. We walked together quietly for about a mile. Putting on and now wearing the yellow jersey changed my mindset completely. We walked several more quiet miles and with each step; my stride improved and I began to feel stronger. We continued this ritual for the next couple of days. I began to look forward to putting on my 'uniform' and my attitude also began to change. The third day he took me for a two-mile bike ride; a duathalon. I put on the yellow jersey and finished. Three days earlier I could hardly walk up steps. Did I change physically in three days? No! It's all up here (in my mind). Put on the yellow jersey! I was in a physical/mental rut. I had to get out and bust my rut. Be a rut-buster and put on the yellow jersey and just do it, whatever IT is. Change your marriage, change your physical program, change your job, change your come home/watch television/eat/sleep Rut. Yes, I have adversity, so what! Yes, there are some things I can't do, like skiing moguls. Physically, I can't do it. But, what *can* I do? I can play Parcheesi, I can bowl, with lots of training, I can ride a bike, and I can discover nice flat walking trails. Find your passion and live as if it were your last chance. This is not a trial run, folks this is the main event.

ACT   List at least one kindness that you will show today to another person as a sign of encouragement.

_____

_____

ACT   List at least one thing that you are passionate about or something that you would change if you knew this was your last chance at life.

_____

_____

Sometimes we need a hero of faith to lift us up so that we can turn around and be a hero of faith for someone else. Keep the cycle of love going and keep on planting! There is a parable in Mark about a mustard seed. It is a small seed that, when watered, grows into a huge tree and gives shade to the birds. We all need a little drink of water at times from God, and from others, so that we can be refreshed and grow. Then go, and do a little "planting" for others.

Lesson Seven: WE ALL HAVE AN ATTITUDE

"We take captive every thought to make it obedient to Christ."
2 Corinthians 10:5

We are all born selfish. We learn from day one to cry when we want food, attention, or changing. Somehow that never seems to stop. We may or may not cry any more, but we find our own way to let people know when we want something. Have you ever wanted something so bad you start bargaining with God? "If you just do this one thing for me, I will never ask for another favor…or, I will be nice to everyone the rest of my life…or, I promise to go back to church." Trust me; bargaining with God does not qualify as an attitude of gratitude. That is whining to get what we want and think we deserve. My friend Julia never whined, she simply was thankful for each and every day.

Millennium New Year's, my dear friend Julia stayed home with a terrible bout with the flu, while I danced the night away somewhere off the coast of Aruba on a 12 day cruise with five other friends. Several weeks later she still had a lingering cough that had apparently moved to her chest, causing what she believed was bronchitis. Upon repeated urgings from friends, she caved under pressure and made a doctor's appointment. She knew antibiotics would kick it out within a few days.

After all, Julia exemplified good health. At age 32, she epitomized good health. She loved to walk, or be walked by her golden retriever, Sam, and enjoyed an occasional hike through the Blue Ridge Mountains or playing tennis with friends. She had a great life. She married a wonderful man and had an ideal job in outside sales with a company car. She and her husband designed a beautiful, unique house with a deck overlooking a pond, possessed financial stability, and had just started trying to have a baby.

Then with one moment in time, her entire world shattered. Well, that's not exactly true. Life would have been shattered for most of us, but not by her definition. To Julia, it was more of a temporary setback that would lead to a new perspective on life. For me, I had the opportunity to witness her "attitude of gratitude" for everything in life. From that day on I noticed her grateful spirit. Life became a journey to be shared and enjoyed with those you love. Just to give you a glimpse of the Julia that I know, and some of that pervasive gratitude, I wanted you to share a little bit of that journey in her own words.

Lesson Seven: WE ALL HAVE AN ATTITUDE

Julia's testimony, given at her church in June of 2000, several months after her cancer diagnosis.

Prayer: Lord, thank you for Your Word, we ask that you minister to us. Thank you for people like Abraham, Paul, and others who acted in faith. Let it not be me who speaks, but You who speaks through me. I pray that the focus is not on my story, but Your words and Your promises. Amen.

To congregation: Pastor Jim asked me to talk to you last month, and I cancelled at the last minute. He threatened to write about me as a lost soul in the church newsletter if I didn't come through, so here I am.

I have had two Scriptures on my desk for a couple of years. When some friends were praying for another friend during her illness, one of the ladies gave these verses to me I have claimed them as mine.

Philippians 4:6 says, "Do not be anxious about anything, but in everything with prayer and petition with thanksgiving, present your requests to God." 1 Thessalonians 5:16-18 says, "Be joyful always, pray continually, and give thanks in all circumstances, for this is God's will for you in Christ Jesus."

Now let's break down the Scriptures. They are perfect for so many of life's occasions; finances, relationships, schooling, illness, etc. These verses are not conditional. They are a command; present your requests to God, be joyful, and pray continually in ALL circumstances.

On a side note; I think it is important that you know Scripture and memorize some verses that are important to you. I have included some of my favorites that I have found helpful to me but if you don't have any of your own, you can borrow mine until you find verses that speak to you.

In January of this year I went to the doctor due to shortness of breath. I asked for antibiotics, but got a lot more than that! I was diagnosed with a rare cancer called Thymoma, Stage four, the latest stage. For those who are medically challenged, like I was, that means it was attached to my thymus gland. I must have had it for several years because it was now the size of a man's fist on my chest bone and had grown into my chest cavity and around my lung.

I left the appointment at which I learned of the cancer. I was scared, holding back tears, and repeating to myself, "Whatever it is, I will beat it, whatever it is, I will beat it, beat it, beat it…" Saying this, I knew I would overcome it. I also knew I couldn't do this by myself. It was time to call in the "Big Gun." I began to pray.

Lesson Seven: WE ALL HAVE AN ATTITUDE

By that night, I felt that I had already given this massive problem to God. I couldn't fix anything myself, so why try? To tell you the truth, I was glad to have the help because I didn't want to have this problem in the first place. I couldn't be anxious about anything because with prayer, lots and lots of prayer and petition, I presented my requests to God. I wasn't joyful yet. I hadn't given thanks for my circumstance yet, but I was getting there.

I had heard a sermon shortly thereafter from Pastor Jim who talked about Abraham having intense faith to do what God had commanded him in Genesis 22. He was asked to sacrifice his son. That was a lot worse than having a tumor! He had to rely fully on God, and trust Him. He didn't talk about his problem with his friends; no emotional dissertation was given, no "woe is me." He just obeyed. God asked him to do this and early the next morning he was off preparing the wood. He was my example of how I should handle my task at hand.

Hebrews 11, talks about the Heroes of Faith. Think about the faith these folks had. Noah put up with the growling, hissing, yapping, teasing from others, and was saved from the flood. Sarah, who was too old and childless, was able to have children. Some of them faced stoning, being sawed in two, and jeered at.

103

Joy Comes in the Morning

Your trials will come in different forms than these heroes of faith. Some will be things you never could have imagined. But God is saying, "I have something infinitely better for you than you can imagine. Do you trust me? Do you believe me? The tests are coming, I promise you, and they will sift your heart." The Lord knows your heart and what you are going through. He asks that you trust Him completely. God offers staggering rewards beyond our comprehension if we obey.

Okay, I got it...having cancer was God's will for me, but how can I be joyful? As I meditated on that verse in Philippians, I had an epiphany and I realized that this was going to be the way I could fulfill a goal of mine. I had never really stepped up to the plate and witnessed my dedication to Jesus Christ to others. Maybe I would talk about it in small groups at church, but I had never really witnessed or gone out to win souls. So when the elders of the church came over and laid hands on me and prayed for healing, I told them that I was *almost* excited. What excited me was the prospect that maybe my having serious cancer was the way I was going to reach out and share the Gospel. It was my course, my path. I had faith. I was joyful and I could give thanks.

But I had one more issue, why? I was led to read about Job and the awful struggle he went through; he lost his family, his wealth, and his health. Job's greatest test was not the pain and suffering, but that he did not know why he had to go through all of that. I really related to that guy! I'd been very healthy; I didn't smoke, I exercised, and I took vitamin C.

So many Christians say, "I'll finish my course", but it is with misery; everyone around them is miserable. They say, "God, why are you doing this to me?" They say, "Okay, if this is God's will, okay, but I want to know *why*, and when I get to heaven I've got some real questions."

I heard this on a tape by Dan McLean, "Here's an idea; if heaven had an arena for those who have questions, it would be packed out to the max. To help answer the questions, there is a committee of people like John the Baptist who got his head cut off, or Isaiah who they believe is the prophet in Hebrews who was sawed in two, Peter who was crucified upside down, Stephen who was stoned to death, Moses who wandered around for 40 years in the wilderness, or maybe like Hannah who was childless. They'll be easy to pick out; John holding his head, Peter upside down, etc."

Can you imagine? "Okay, Julia is up next to ask your question." "Okay, I wanna' know why I got a tumor." John would comment, "What did she say? I lost my head and you are crying about a tumor." Isaiah says, "I'm still trying to get up." You get my point, I think.

Our greatest test may be that we trust God's goodness even though we don't understand why our lives are going a certain way. We must learn to trust in a God that is good and not in the goodness of life. There will never be a place that God will lead you that the grace of God cannot keep you.

In summary, my University of Arizona ape (a small toy ape that plays the fight song when you press his hand) is kind of like faith. It was a gift from my dad and my step mom from Arizona. You are faced with this scary, hairy, seemingly awful "gift", but you give thanks for it. Then it is your decision, you hide your scary gift in a box, or, you take the gift by the hand, not sure what you're going to get out of it. All of a sudden, when you squeeze the ape's hand, it plays music (albeit the Arizona fight song), cheers you on, and it dances. The gift I thought was awfully scary plays you a pep rally and brings you so much joy! We played that silly ape every morning in the hospital while getting chemo; when I would wake up to another day and say, "Good morning, nurses! Room 6508 is up"! We have had more fun with this "scary gift" than any other gifts I have received to date.

It is kind of like me having cancer. I have had one of the most blessed years ever. Isn't it funny how the same year

Lesson Seven: WE ALL HAVE AN ATTITUDE

I find out I have cancer is the same year I read the Bible for the first time? Isn't it funny how the same year I get cancer, is the first year I've noticed redbuds – how do you not notice redbuds? I've passed by them every year for ten years and never noticed beautiful purple flowered trees. Because of my scary gift of cancer, I have gotten to spend really good quality time with my family and friends – hung out with them for weeks at a time – gone rappelling, rock climbing, kayaking, and swam with dolphins. We are leaving Wednesday for a trip to Europe. One of my dreams was to take my mom to Bath, England. I don't know if we would have gotten around to doing that if it weren't for my situation.

Yes, I am giving you the highlights. It is not all fun and games. I don't want to make light of any situation. I've backslid a lot into self-pity; I haven't gotten to start a family yet, and I have only been married for 6 years. I'm not done loving Mid, but when are you ever done loving someone? There are folks in this room who are going through unspeakable sorrow. But our "courses" are what they are. If we hold dear to what God is telling us or commanding us; if we walk in faith, not sight, His glory and goodness will be revealed.

Sometimes we want someone else's course. We tried ours but it didn't work. I'll take Door Number Two. Let's get on with whatever the course is. If this is it, I don't want to miss any blessing that comes with it. I want to finish my course, and finish it with joy. Give thanks in all circumstances, for this is God's will for you in Christ Jesus.

I want to close with a poem by Amy Carmichael of India. Amy Carmichael suffered neuralgia, a disease of the nerves that made her whole body weak and achy and often put her in bed for weeks on end. It was at the Keswick Convention of 1887 that she heard Hudson Taylor speak about missionary life. Soon afterward, she became convinced of her calling to missionary work.

> Hast thou no scar?
>
> No hidden scar on foot, or side, or hand?
>
> I hear thee sung as mighty in the land,
>
> I hear them hail thy bright ascendant star:
>
> Hast though no scar?
>
> Hast though no wound?
>
> Yet, I was wounded by the archers, spent.
>
> Leaned me against the tree to die, and rent.
>
> By ravening beasts that compassed me, I swooned:
>
> Hast thou no wound?

No wound? No scar?

Yes, as the master shall the servant be,

And pierced are the feet that follow me.

But Thine are whole. Can he have followed far?

Who has no wound? No scar?

Prayer: There are some here with great questions, great sorrow. Jesus reveal your glory and let them realize that the sufferings of the present aren't even worthy of the glory that will be revealed. Lord, let our lives be yours. Amen.

ASK   In what area do you struggle with an attitude of gratitude? Stop and thank the Lord anyway for your situation, whether you feel it or not.

_____

_____

Julia woke up each day and put on the amour of God (Refer to Lesson One, Page 9, Ephesians 6:13-17) to give her the strength to have a victorious day, one day at a time. What a blessing we would be to others if we all lived each day as if it were our last, with an attitude of gratitude. I have attempted to live in a manner that would honor Julia and her

Joy Comes in the Morning

life every day that I am privileged to live on this earth. I know that I am not always successful, I am mindful in knowing that I am extremely grateful for the time I had with Julia as my friend and that good friends are truly a gift from God. I know that I am grateful that the Lord has blessed me more than I could have ever hoped or imagined with a wonderful husband, family and friends, yes, even with material things. When I start to want more "stuff" or am feeling a little unloved or frustrated by those around me, I stop and notice God's amazing creation and all He has given me. He has given me a real love story, a fairy tale with a happy ending. By persevering through my life's challenges I now know for a fact that Joy truly does come in the morning!

ACT

Open the bible and memorize a verse about thankfulness and repeat to the group or to yourself in the mirror. Write verse here.

_____

_____

_____

Lesson Seven: *WE ALL HAVE AN ATTITUDE*

List 10 things you are thankful for right now:

1. _____

2. _____

3. _____

4. _____

5. _____

6. _____

7. _____

8. _____

9. _____

10. _____

Lesson Eight: THE VICTORY DANCE

"The LORD God is in your midst, A victorious warrior. He will exult over you with joy, He will be quiet in His love, He will rejoice over you with shouts of joy."
Zephaniah 3:17

"My times are in Your hand."
Psalm 31:15

Jim Valvano led the North Carolina State University basketball team to a national championship before he became a sports broadcaster. Then cancer developed in his lower back. This is what he had to say about it, "Life changes when you least expect it to. The future is uncertain. So, seize this day, seize this moment, and make the most of it." We all need to seize the day, every day.

"(For God) has turned for me my mourning into dancing." (Psalm 30:11) I have adopted this as my life verse for I have seen God do this in my life, Julia's life, and the life of others time and time again. He has taken my heartache and taught me joy in the midst of suffering. This makes my heart dance.

God did the same for Joseph in the book of Genesis when Joseph's brothers were jealous of him and sold him into slavery they left him for dead…God meant it for good. Joseph was purchased by Potiphar, an Egyptian officer of Pharaoh, and "the Lord was with Joseph, so he became a successful man." The Lord caused all Joseph did to prosper, so Potiphar made Joseph overseer of his entire house and all that he owned. When Potiphar's wife looked at Joseph with desire, he held fast to his integrity and refused to be with her. She plotted to have him thrown in jail. Once again Joseph was wronged for no reason. After several years in prison, Pharaoh inquired for someone to interpret his dreams and Joseph was able to accurately give account to him. Pharaoh began to trust him and Joseph became Prime Minister, second only to Pharaoh. He rose again to a position of great authority and prepared for years of famine in the land that God had warned him about. When Joseph's brothers came to ask for food, we witness an amazing act of mercy and forgiveness.

Do you ever feel like Joseph? Wrongly accused or tossed aside? Dare to dream that God wants to bless you, because He does.

Lesson Eight: THE VICTORY DANCE

ASK

What does victory mean to you? Describe a victory in your life:

_____

_____

My passion is dancing. I started performing in dance recitals starting at the age of 3. My parents attended every dance recital and continued to attend my 'shows' into my 30's with ballroom dance competitions. Julia and Mid also took ballroom dancing lessons. I remember Julia telling the story of dancing at one of the studio parties and she turned her head to the left to look over Mid's shoulder so she could be in proper dance position. Upon turning her head to the left the wig did not turn with her head, so she found herself looking at her hair. She believed you had to be able to laugh at yourself no matter what.

Another one of my favorite stories about Julia is losing her hair in chemotherapy. The first round of treatments resulted in loss of her beautiful brunette, shoulder length hair. Once again, Julia refused to be depressed by this event. She marched in to her hairdresser and promptly asked for a Mohawk. After taking several pictures, which I can assure you were not pretty, and a lot of laughs, she had them shave the Mohawk off too. Then she promptly purchased a brunette wig that went to her shoulders, a platinum blonde wig and a long curly redhead wig. An evening out consisted of everyone wearing one of Julia's wigs. To her relief, her hair eventually grew back, shorter and curlier than before, but at least it was her hair. Then she was preparing once again to lose her hair for the next round of treatments. Not long after completing round two of chemo, three of her friends showed up at her door…with their heads shaved to show their support for Julia. The irony was Julia never lost her hair! Well, at least they all got their picture in the paper.

I tell that story to show Julia's sense of humor but also the love she felt for her friends and vice versa. Julia showed everyone she met such love that most of her friends would do anything possible to return the favor. Julia lived her life reflecting the self-less love of Christ as demonstrated in John 13:4-5, when Jesus washes the feet of His disciples. **1 John 4:7 (NIV) says, "Dear friends, let us continue to love one another, for love comes from God. Anyone who loves is born of God and knows God."**

During Julia's memorial ceremony seven years later, which we refer to as her praise service, since that was what her life was all about, her husband said these words, "Her spiritual gift was making others feel better about THEMSELVES after being with her. What a special gift!

She LOVED people…ALL people…in the 17 years I knew her, I never heard her say a negative word about anyone. ANYONE! In all that physical suffering she NEVER LET IT AFFECT HER ATTITUDE OR SPIRIT!" She lived her life verse of, **"Give thanks in ALLLLLLLL circumstances, for this is God's will for you in Christ Jesus" (1 Thessalonians 5:18 (NIV)).** I stub my baby toe clipping a chair and MAN I get an attitude!"

Julia's life dance on this earth may have ended, but we must continue to dance.

When I am actually physically dancing, the rest of the world fades away. I am focused and challenged. Ballroom Dancing provides a sense of accomplishment for me and stress relief. God wants to have that effect on us too. Spending time with Him should make the rest of the world fade away. Living for Christ is a daily choice and it will be challenging at times. If we remain focused on the victory we have in Christ, there is a calming effect and a sense of accomplishment that we can't find anywhere else. We try, though. We buy things and travel and compete to be the best and have the best of everything in order to find ultimate peace. It never works. There is a void that can only be filled by God.

Joy Comes in the Morning

I love the words from a song that says, "When you can't see His hand, trust His heart." We must look past the storms of life raging all around us and fix our eyes on Heaven. Then we will not be mired down and deceived into believing that God does not care. We must trust; Faith, not feelings; character, not circumstances. Our feelings will deceive us. One day we feel good, the other not so good. One day we feel happy and the other we are mad. One day we feel love for another person and the next day we don't. Feelings lie and they let us down. Rely on faith and not feelings. Faith in what we KNOW to be true, Faith in God's Word, and not how we feel right now.

Similarly, our character should remain the same regardless of the circumstances, not change with the wind. **"Consider it joy when you encounter various trials. Knowing that the testing of your faith produces endurance. And let endurance have its perfect result, that you may be perfect and complete, lacking in nothing. But if any of you lacks wisdom, let him ask of God who gives to all men freely and without reproach, and it will be given to him. And when you ask, ask without doubting, for the one who doubts is like the surf of the sea, directionless and being tossed by the wind." (James 1:2-6)**

Lesson Eight: THE VICTORY DANCE

I had another friend who went through several months of chemo and radiation for cancer in 2005. She came through with flying colors. During that time she sent an email devotion that I thought I would share with you about Guidance. The author is said to be anonymous, but it is a beautiful devotion and meant to be shared.

Title: <u>Dancing With God</u>

When I meditated on the word GUIDANCE, I kept seeing "dance" at the end of the word. I remember reading that doing God's will is a lot like dancing. When two people try to lead, nothing feels right. The movement doesn't flow with the music, and everything is quite uncomfortable and jerky. When one person realizes and lets the other lead, both bodies begin to flow with the music. One gives gentle cues, perhaps with a nudge to the back or by pressing lightly in one direction or another. It's as if two become one body moving beautifully. The dance takes surrender, willingness and attentiveness from one person, as well as gentle guidance and skill from the other. My eyes drew back to the word GUIDANCE. When I saw "G" I thought of God, followed by U and I. God, you, and I dance. This statement is what guidance means to me. As I lowered my head, I became willing to trust that I would get guidance about my life.

Once again, I became willing to let God lead. My prayer for you today is that God's blessings and mercies are upon you and your loved ones on this day and every day. May you abide in Him as He abides in you. Dance together with God, trusting Him to lead and to guide you through each season of your life.

Kudos to the author of that poem.

<u>DANCE</u>!!

<u>D</u>evoted to prayer

<u>A</u>ttitude of gratitude

<u>N</u>ever give up

<u>C</u>ommitted in Love

<u>E</u>njoy the Victory

I am not sure if I can adequately explain victory. It is something I wish I had understood years before. It would have saved me so much heartache. **"Thanks be to God, who gives us *Victory* in the Lord, Christ Jesus. Therefore, my beloved brethren, be steadfast, immoveable, always abounding in your work for the Lord, knowing that your toil is not in vain in the Lord." (1 Corinthians 15: 57-58)** The words "steadfast and immoveable" jump out at me.

Lesson Eight: *THE VICTORY DANCE*

Whether at work or personal, we are called to be steadfast and immoveable in trusting the Lord. That is how to gain victory over adversity. When times are tough, 'DANCE!' Devote yourself to a powerful prayer life, maintain an attitude of gratitude, and never give up. Stay committed until you overcome adversity and enjoy the victory! DANCE!

ASK
How can you share in someone else's victory?

_____

_____

ASK
What is one main take-a-way you have from reading this book? In other words; one life lesson learned about overcoming adversity that leads to joy in the morning.

_____

_____

Julia never said she was battling cancer. She always said it was her dance in life. She dared to dream of beating the odds, and she dreamed of traveling abroad and accomplishing grand things. She always prayed and never gave up. Her commitment to God never wavered, and her commitment to continuing her dance was relentless. She fully expected victory in every area of her life. She received victory in her friendships, with a wonderful spouse, financially, by achieving many goals, and in surviving seven years beyond the doctors' expectations. With God's help she was victorious until the day He chose to take her home and I know He said to Julia, "well done, my good and faithful servant." Now he has given her gifts and glory beyond measure. He has made her well and given her a new, healthy, and perfect body. Julia danced and now she is dancing with Jesus our savior! With every new day I am reminded of Julia and how her life and words will stay with me forever. My life has been forever changed by living a life knowing that no matter what; Joy Comes in the Morning.

About the Author
Sherri K. Baldwin

Sherri Baldwin is the Principal of LeadAdvantage, Inc., a leadership and team development company. Sherri has had the privilege of providing leadership development to companies both in the US and internationally.

Sherri has a Bachelor of Arts degree in Communications from Texas A&M University and continues to serve on the Leadership Council. She is a Distinguished Toastmaster and a certified coach in the WorkPlace Big Five Personality Profile. Sherri also participates in several local displaced volunteer projects such Lois' Lodge and Nexus. Sherri and her husband attend Forest Hills Church in Charlotte, NC where they have been blessed to hear pastor, Dr. David Chadwick for over 20 years.

sherri@leadadvantageinc.com

CPSIA information can be obtained at www.ICGtesting.com
Printed in the USA
LVOW012153021011

248797LV00008B/133/P